The New Science Teacher's Handbook

Studymates

25 Key Topics in Business Studies
25 Key Topics in Human Resources
25 Key Topics in Marketing
Accident & Emergency Nursing
Business Organisation
Cultural Studies
English Legal System
European Reformation
Genetics
Hilter & Nazi Germany
Land Law
Organic Chemistry
Practical Drama & Theatre Arts
Revolutionary Conflicts
Social Anthropology
Social Statistics
Speaking Better French
Speaking English
Studying Chaucer
Studying History
Studying Literature
Studying Poetry
Understanding Maths

Many other titles in preparation

The New Science Teacher's Handbook

John Guttridge
BSc(Hons); MRSC, PGCE

www.**studymates**.co.uk

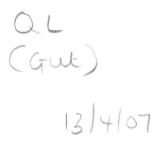

7508311249

First published in 2003 by Studymates Limited, PO Box 2 Bishops Lydeard, Somerset TA4 3YE,
United Kingdom.

Telephone: (01823) 432002
Fax: (01823) 430097
Website: http://www.studymates.co.uk

Typeset by PDQ Typesetting, Newcastle-under-Lyme
Printed and bound in Great Britain by The Baskerville Press Ltd.

Contents

List of illustrations   vii

Biographical note on the author   viii

Preface   ix

1 The Science Department: Organisation and Policies   1
One-minute summary   *1*
Organisation   1
Policies   4
Summary   7

2 The Curriculum   8
One-minute summary   *8*
The National Curriculum   8
Key Stage 3   8
Key Stage 4   14
Post-16 education   16
Schemes of work   19
Summary   19

3 Teaching and Learning   20
One-minute summary   *20*
The accelerated learning cycle   20
Creating the learning environment   21
Other aspects of teaching and learning   25
Literacy and numeracy   28
Gifted and talented students   28
Multiple intelligences   29
Emotional intelligence   31
Summary   31

4 Discipline   32
One-minute summary   *32*
The classroom discipline plan   32
Ten tips for success   38
Summary   40

5 A Good Science Lesson   41
One-minute summary   *41*
Before the lesson   42
The start of the lesson   43
Part 1 of the lesson – the introduction   43
Part 2 of the lesson – the main activity   44
Part 3 of the lesson – the plenary session   46

A word about health and safety   47
A typical lesson plan using the three-part structure   47
Summary   50

6 Organising your Paperwork and Time   52
One-minute summary   *52*
Coping with the paper mountain   52
Handling post   57
Time management   57
Assessment and planning   57
Summary   59

7 Good Demonstrations   60
One-minute summary   *60*
A good demonstration   60
Before you start   60
During the demonstration   61
After the demonstration   62
An example of a demonstration   62
Summary   64

8 Professional Development   65
One-minute summary   *65*
The career entry profile   65
Your induction year   66
Further professional development   68
Performance management   69
Summary

9 Pastoral Care and Parents   70
One-minute summary   *70*
Your tutor group   70
Parents' evenings   72
Summary   72

10 Using Computers   73
One-minute summary   *73*
What can I expect?   73
How are computers used in science lessons?   74
You and computers   76
What about the future?   76
Summary   76

11 Useful Websites   77

Appendices   79

Index   123

List of illustrations

1 The departmental hierarchy   1

2 Attainment levels during each year of Key Stage 3   13

3 The accelerated learning cycle   20

4 A typical worksheet for the example lesson   49

5 A useful layout for a planner   53

6 A section of a typical mark book   54

Biographical Note on the Author

John Guttridge BSc(Hons) MRSC PGCE graduated in chemistry at the University of Surrey and completed his post-graduate studies at the University of Wales, Cardiff. He joined the Royal Society of Chemistry in 1978. He has more than 25 years' teaching, 16 years' public examining and over 15 years' experience as a Head of Department with responsibility for tutoring many teachers and newly qualified teachers in science. He is currently the Specialist Science College Co-ordinator at the St Augustine of Canterbury School, Taunton, Somerset.

Preface

Teaching must be one of the most rewarding professions in the world. The good teacher not only has the responsibility for educating the future of humankind but he or she will find it an enjoyable, if not stressful, experience! Moreover, a good teacher is always remembered with affection by his or her students – good teachers often end up with countless friends for life. This book is designed for those of you who are thinking of becoming a science teacher, for those of you who are starting your training courses, or for those who are in their first years of employment in a science department. This book will be of benefit primarily to yet-to-qualify or newly qualified science teachers at secondary level, but should also benefit teachers with a direct responsibility for science at Key Stage 2. It will provide teachers and student teachers with a wealth of basic information necessary for the smooth transition into the teaching profession (and beyond) both for the young newly-qualified teacher and the student teacher, whether a young college leaver or a more mature person seeking a career change. The emphasis is on the *professional* approach to teaching and not on a handbook full of quick-fix remedies for a 'failing' teacher. May I welcome you to the profession and wish you every success in the future.

John Guttridge BSc(Hons): MRSC; PGCE

The Science Department: Organisation and Policies

One-minute summary – In this chapter we will look at the typical science department in a secondary school, how it is organised, and the structures within it. In addition, the chapter deals with how science is taught – whether to classes of mixed ability, or by setting children according to their ability in the subject – and the respective merits of both systems. Finally, what makes a good departmental handbook is discussed, and the need to adhere to departmental policies.

Organisation

Department staff

The most common form of hierarchical organisation within a science department involves a head of science, responsible for the three science disciplines, each of which may have a departmental head. Unfortunately, all science departments are different – some may have only three or four teaching staff plus one or two technicians. Others may be very large – 15–20 teaching staff in a large comprehensive, plus a team of technicians. For the sake of simplicity, we will assume that the department is of moderate size, in a school of about 1,000 students. There are nine teaching staff, and a team of four technicians. The likely method of organising is shown in Figure 1.

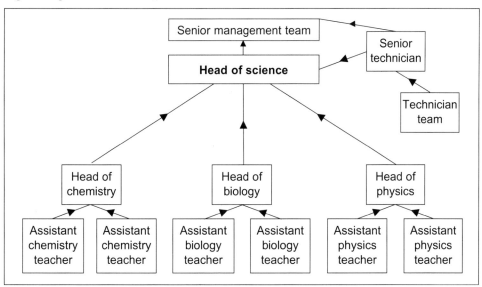

Figure 1. The departmental hierarchy.

As you can see from the diagram, the assistant teachers in each discipline are responsible to, and line managed by, the head of each subject. Similarly, each head of subject is responsible to the head of science who, in turn, is directly responsible to the senior management team. In smaller schools, the heads of each discipline may be omitted and a second-in-charge of science is present instead. In small schools there may only be the head of science plus the assistant teachers of each subject. As a newly qualified teacher you may be appointed as an assistant teacher in one of the science subjects. Promotion after the appropriate amount of experience would come either in this structure, or in the pastoral system (see Chapter 8).

The technical staff in the department have their own hierarchical structure. The assistant technicians are responsible to and line managed by the senior technician, who is in turn responsible to the head of department, but in some schools the senior technician is responsible to the head of non-teaching staff, who may double as the bursar, or the head teacher's personal assistant. Other posts within larger departments may also be present: head of Key Stage 3 science, head of Key Stage 4 science, head of sixth form science, head of special needs (science) and so on.

Curriculum

Curriculum organisation depends on the school. Although the National Curriculum is the mandatory science curriculum in this country, the method of delivery can be varied. There are various aspects to consider when looking at the curriculum organisation of a science department; these include:

Mixed ability vs setting or streaming

The debate as to which is the most effective method of teaching i.e. mixed ability or grouping by ability, continues to grow unabated. Each method has its advantages and disadvantages. Mixed ability teaching, for example, needs a totally different style of delivery from teaching ability groups for effective learning. Differentiation needs to be far more defined, resources chosen appropriately and carefully, and marking, target setting and assessment policies need to be looked at in a new light. It is imperative to realise that a style that may suit some staff and students in one situation will be disastrous in another. In ability groups, differentiation is still important (don't forget that you will still have a spread of ability even in a tightly setted class) but the range of ability will be much less. It may be easier to pitch the delivery of a lesson to such a class. However, organising in this way means that students who underachieve because of behavioural problems rather than learning problems often find themselves together in the same sets, thus increasing the risk of less-motivated classes and all the problems that that can bring. However, in the end, how you will be delivering the curriculum is a question of which style is accepted in the department in which you find yourself.

Separate science subjects vs combined science
Again, there are advantages and disadvantages to each system. In many schools, all science is taught as combined science to all pupils. In this scenario you would be expected to teach biology, chemistry and physics up to GCSE level. The obvious advantage over this system is that by seeing students in your classes frequently you get to know the students very well, with all that that implies regarding target setting, report writing and so on. Many teachers rise to the challenge of teaching a discipline where they perhaps have fewer skills. The disadvantages include the preparation time needed to cope with unfamiliar subject content – time which could be spent more profitably in other areas, and the possibility that those sciences outside your immediate speciality are not taught quite as well as your specialised subject.

Where science is taught as individual subjects, the obvious advantage is that specialist teachers are able to teach their subject, bringing into their teaching all the experiences and anecdotal extras that spice up a lesson. Also, the introduction of specialist subjects means that those students going on to A level and beyond already have a clear understanding of what constitutes 'chemistry', 'physics' and 'biology'. In this set-up, however, there will be less contact with individual classes by the specialist teacher, and so there will be obvious problems about getting to know the class well, and also with continuity in the curriculum.

In practice, most schools adopt a mixture of the above. Combined science is taught to years 7 and 8 (and possibly 9 as well) with year 10 splitting into specialist subjects in a co-ordinated (three separate subjects) science GCSE syllabus. This system has the advantage that you can get to know the students lower down in the school, with the added advantage of specialist teachers at Key Stages 4 and 5.

Timetable blocking vs backing with other subjects
In many schools science groups are grouped according to ability. This is either by streaming or by setting. Streaming means that particular students are put into ability groups and it is within these groups that they are taught for a variety of subjects. Each subject involved in the streaming system is backed against the others. In small schools where setting is impractical or impossible, streaming is the next best method of ability grouping. Setting, however, is more flexible in that students are placed in ability groups depending upon the subject, and that individual subjects or groups of subjects are set independently of others. This means that a student could be in set 1 for, say, mathematics, but could be in set 2 for science and set 3 for English. This system is only effective, however, if the sets in an individual subject are blocked; i.e. all the science lessons in a particular year group are timetabled at the same time. This is usually only possible in certain size schools where the number of laboratories equals or exceeds the number of sets in a year group. The advantage with blocking is, of course, that a department has full control over setting within that department – movement of students between groups, as a result of progress, is possible without affecting other subject areas.

Policies

On joining a science department, the departmental scheme of work or handbook is the most important document that needs to be referred to throughout your induction year and beyond. All department handbooks should contain the following:

- ▶ Science rationale.
- ▶ Science department aims and objectives.
- ▶ Staffing deployment within the department including job descriptions of both teaching and support staff (e.g. technicians).
- ▶ Science department development plan.
- ▶ Science department work plan.
- ▶ Teachers' timetables.
- ▶ Policies on homework, marking, and other major areas.
- ▶ Complete scheme of work for each Key Stage, including risk assessments and resources.

It is important that you obtain the department handbook as soon as possible after joining the school, or even before joining. Read it carefully, especially the policies and procedures section, so that you can face your first class with confidence knowing that you are implementing the department procedures in such a way that if problems arise, then appropriate support from senior staff is that much easier to obtain. In this section we will take each of the above areas in turn.

- ▶ **Science rationale**. Every science department handbook should have a short rationale. This section declares the philosophy of the department in a concise, succinct way. A candidate for interview can often discover a lot about a department in a short time by reading this section.

- ▶ **Science department aims and objectives**. Here the broad aims and more detailed objectives are laid out. A good department will ensure that good science is taught well to *all* pupils meaning that, as well as special needs students and exceptionally able students, the average student is not overlooked – all too easy to do in a busy comprehensive school.

- ▶ **Staffing deployment within the department including job descriptions of both teaching and support staff (e.g. technicians).** Good departments ensure that every member knows their responsibilities. This includes support staff such as laboratory technicians and learning support assistants if they are allocated specifically to the science department. Departments that include all teaching and non-teaching staff in decision and policy making are usually successful, as each member, including the newest newly qualified teacher is valued and willing to give of his or her best. Look out for this.

▶ **Science department development plan.** This shows the direction in which the department is heading. Good departments will have a clear development plan, with the emphasis on development, rather than maintenance of current practice. Do not be impressed, however, with a plan that includes a plethora of ideas and intentions for the next year or so. Such departments are seldom able to achieve their targets. Instead, look for a plan that shows just three or four ideas that are properly costed in terms of time, finances and other resources, and which have a set date by when they need to be achieved, with the criteria for success clearly laid out.

▶ **Science department work plan.** Sadly, in schools today, there is a great deal of under-funding. However, successful departments will use their limited resources as wisely as possible. If there is one set of expensive equipment in the department (for example, microscopes) then the handbook should contain a rota system for such equipment. If some year groups are block timetables (meaning that all the five classes in a particular, say, five-stream year group are taught at the same time in five different laboratories), then it is of prime importance that clashes do not take place. Good departments will have a system for dealing with this. One method is that the work throughout the academic year is taught in free-standing modules, staggered so that they are taught at different times of the year. The students all do the complete syllabus, but in a different order. At various times (say, halfway through the year and/or at the end of the academic year), they will have all covered the same topics so that comparative assessment and also movement between groups can take place.

▶ **Teachers' timetables.** This is not particularly vital, but the complete timetable of each department member is useful, especially when arranging meetings or lesson observation in non-contact periods. Occasionally, if a newly qualified teacher is unable to observe particular classes taken by the head of department because non-contact periods and the particular class do not coincide, one glance at the department timetable may show, for example, that the second in department is free when that class is being taught by the head of department, so that the second in department can then cover the newly qualified teacher's lesson, freeing him or her to observe the class.

▶ **Policies on homework, marking, and other major areas.** All department handbooks need to have a large number of policy statements. More than this, each member needs to know what they are and abide by them. This will enable the head of department to answer parents' concerns over homework, detentions and so on, with much more of a degree of authority. If a department member does not adhere to department policy on some matters, it is often difficult and embarrassing in parental interviews if the department is seen not to be consistent. Consistency is a quality to look for when reading and experiencing department policies. A good department handbook should have clear, concise policies on a large number of aspects relevant to science. The following list is not exhaustive, but covers the main areas. Some of the policies are of prime importance and are therefore covered separately elsewhere in this book:

absent teachers and work set	newly qualified teachers
accidents	progression
assessment	record of achievement
capitation and finances	recording
career opportunities	reporting
charging policy (e.g. breakages)	resources and their uses
communication with parents	sex education
cross curricular links	staff monitoring
differentiation	staff development
discipline	student teachers
displays	target setting
equal opportunities	teaching styles
evaluation of scheme of work	technical language and spelling
health and safety	time management
homework	use of calculators
lesson observation	use of ICT
liaison (primary, FE, industry)	use of library/resource centre
links with other areas	use of technicians and learning support
meetings	assistants
monitoring progress	word processing of students' work.

▶ **Complete scheme of work for each Key Stage including risk assessments and resources.** Many schools are now adopting the new QCA scheme of work that can be downloaded free from the Standards website (see Chapter 11) If a department decides that it needs its own scheme then there are a number of areas that need to be included for each lesson or group of lessons:

prior knowledge	assessment opportunities
subject matter	resources, including AV aids
concepts that need to be addressed	opportunities for addressing and
desired outcome	assessing Sc1
teaching styles/methods/suggestions	opportunities for addressing and
ideas for homework	assessing ICT
ideas for differentiation	risk Assessment

A good department should address all these points in their scheme of work. If a department that you are working in is using their own scheme, make sure that these areas are included. If not, it is essential that you include these items in your own lesson plans, especially if you are to be observed by your tutor or line manager.

Summary

Science departments vary, but in this chapter we have looked at how a typical department may be structured. However, there are certain areas where all departments should be similar. The most important of these is that the handbook should contain all that is good practice. Most of all, a good handbook must be put into practice. This is one of the most important things to remember in good science teaching.

2

The Curriculum

One-minute summary – This chapter is devoted to exploring the National Curriculum at Key Stages 3 and 4 and the science courses available for the public examinations at GCSE and post-16.

The National Curriculum

All state schools in the United Kingdom, by law, (and many independent schools by choice) follow the National Curriculum for science. Key Stage 1 covers the first years at school up to the age of 7 (i.e. year 3). Key Stage 2 builds on Key Stage 1 and is targeted at pupils up to the age of 11 (year 6). At Secondary level, Key Stage 3 science is taught to students up to the age of 14 (year 9). Key Stage 4 completes compulsory schooling and finishes at the end of year 11. Science is compulsory at all Key Stages unless, for very special reasons, the student is disapplied. The National Curriculum lays down, through programmes of study, the content and key skills of what is to be taught at each Key Stage. As this book will be dealing primarily with the secondary science teacher, we will concentrate mostly on Key Stages 3 and beyond.

Key Stage 3

The complete scheme of work as approved by the Qualifications and Curriculum Authority (QCA) can be downloaded as a PDF file from the Standards website (see Chapter 11). The scheme is split into three years, 7, 8 and 9, with a complete scheme for each year. In each year the curriculum is split further into several **units** each of which covers a particular topic. The units are arranged in such a way that many topics are revisited each year and are taught at different depths in what is known as a 'spiral curriculum'. Thus students' knowledge and understanding is revised and reinforced each year.

Each unit contains sections guiding the teacher about the breadth and depth at which a topic is taught.

(a) **About the unit**. This provides the main learning objectives for the students. These make good learning objectives to share with the students at the start of the appropriate lessons. However, some will need the English to be at a level appropriate to the student's ages, and so some interpretation by the teacher will be necessary.

(b) **Where the unit fits in**. This section puts the particular unit in context. This is very useful for the teacher as it provides cross-topic links to other areas of the curriculum. Students will find learning easier if they are able to see patterns in the topics they are covering.

(c) **Expectations**. Not all students will achieve the highest standards in science. Some, of course, will, whilst others will learn at a slower rate. In this section the expectations of what most students will achieve are clearly laid out. Also, differentiation is achieved by stating what slower learners will have achieved, and also what more able students will have achieved over and above the normal requirements.

(d) **Prior learning**. This is very useful for the teacher as it provides some ideas regarding the prior knowledge of a class at the start of the topic, and also shows up areas of weakness if this is used as a basis of initial questions in the preliminary part of a lesson.

(e) **Health and safety**. Risk assessments are provided for any potentially hazardous practical activity.

(f) **Language for learning**. Literacy (and numeracy, for that matter) in science is a major issue. In this section issues regarding literacy in science are mentioned, along with ideas that could be implemented.

(g) **Resources**. The main resources needed are outlined in this section, so that teachers and technicians can plan in advance what is needed and when. For example, many schools have one set of dataloggers that will be shared among all the classes at Key Stages 3 and 4, and so early booking will be essential. Knowing what you will need in the medium- to long-term will help to avoid booking clashes.

(h) **Out of school learning**. Opportunities for trips or fieldwork are suggested in this section. It is up to the individual department or teacher to decide which activities, if any, are appropriate to a particular group of students.

For each spread in the scheme of work there are the main objectives for each lesson, suggested activities and learning outcomes. These will be dealt with in more detail in Chapter 5.

Key Stage 3 National Strategy
This is a government initiative designed to raise achievement in all secondary schools. The strategy promotes eight basic principles:

1. Sufficient teaching time – not only for the teaching and learning of knowledge, but also the understanding and skills related to scientific enquiry and method.

2. Direct teaching by the classroom teacher, using whole-class teaching as well as groupwork, including the demonstration of practical skills.

3. The skilful use of differentiation in the classroom so that all pupils are engaged on task.

4. Appropriate extra support for those students who need it to maintain the standards of the rest of a cohort.

5. Opportunities to develop scientific language through oral work and mental skills by the use of modelling.

6. Opportunities for students to use and apply their understanding of key scientific skills with support if appropriate.

7. Opportunities to carry out investigative work, (not simply practical work), whenever appropriate.

8. Reflection time for students to review their achievements.

The strategy comes with time available for schools to undertake training by external advisers appointed specially to enable the strategy to succeed.

Key scientific skills
Key skills are an essential part of the Key Stage 3 National Strategy (see principle 6 above). These skills are taught either discretely, or as part of the everyday scientific education – whichever is appropriate.

1. Communication
This skill is probably the most essential of all. Pupils need to develop skills in listening, speaking and discussing. Their responses to questions using appropriate scientific vocabulary, either to the teacher or as part of group work are a major part of this skill. Other skills involve observing; describing and explaining, recording; reading to obtain or extract information; summarising; writing reports, drawing diagrams, charts or posters.

2. Number application
Science teaching contributes a great deal to numeracy across the curriculum. Examples of where number skills are needed include counting; measuring, estimating values; recording results; working with formulae or equations;

calculating, and, one of the most important skills – plotting and interpreting graphs.

3. Information technology
The use of ICT in science is limited to the facilities available in a department or school. However, the following examples should be well within the scope of most establishments – searching for information in databases, CD-ROMs or the Internet; datalogging; developing spreadsheets; storing information; presenting graphical data, and presenting written reports.

4. Working with others in a group
In science practical activities, this skill is evident in many ways. Examples include the sharing of ideas, following safe working methods and in assembling information from secondary sources.

5. Improving the students' own learning and performance
Pupils need to have many opportunities to reflect on their achievements. For example, they need to improve their own work or test answers, and to check their progress as they progress through units. They need to review and evaluate what they did and how they could improve it. This can be achieved by the students setting targets at the start of a topic, and checking that they have met them at the end.

6. Problem solving
As students progress in scientific enquiry, they begin to develop the skill of problem solving. Examples of this kind of activity include analysing and interpreting information; applying ideas; weighing up evidence and selecting suitable apparatus. 'Egg race' activities carried out at the end of term can help to improve this skill.

7. Thinking skills
Thinking skills enable students to answer the question 'how?' as well as the question 'what?'. The following thinking skills complement the key skills and should pervade all the units at Key Stage 3:

▶ **Information processing skills** – enable students to sort, classify, sequence, compare and contrast relevant information.

▶ **Reasoning skills** – enable students to draw inferences and make deductions, to use precise language and to make reasoned judgements.

▶ **Enquiry skills** – enable students to ask relevant questions, to plan what to do and how to research, to predict and to test conclusions.

▶ **Creative thinking skills** – enable students to generate and extend ideas, to suggest hypotheses and to accept that there may be alternative outcomes.

▶ **Evaluation skills** – enable the student to judge the value of what they read, hear and do, and to develop skills of judgment of others' work.

Programme of study

This may be found on the Standards website (see Chapter 11) along with the QCA scheme of work. The programme of study gives the content that is required to be taught at Key Stage 3. The statements are very broad in some areas and a little open to interpretation, especially where special needs students are concerned. However, it is important that the teacher uses his or her professional judgment to balance the need for relevance for the student and the need to be inclusive. The Programme of Study is divided into four sections, roughly equivalent to practical skills, biology, chemistry and physics.

▶ **Sc1 – Scientific enquiry.** Contains the content that relates to practical scientific skills in the laboratory. For example, students need to be taught how to make predictions, to plan investigations, to decide on the range of values to be observed, to observe and measure accurately, to present results as graphs or charts, to interpret results and draw conclusions and to evaluate their work and suggest ways of improving it.

▶ **Sc2 – Life processes and living things.** This is the main biology content of the Key Stage 3 curriculum. This is split into sections on cells, the human body, plants, variation, classification, inheritance and the environment.

▶ **Sc3 – Materials and their properties.** This corresponds to the chemistry part of the programme of study. Three main areas are studied – classifying materials, changing materials and patterns of behaviour.

▶ **Sc4 – Physical Processes.** This is the Physics part of the programme. The topics here include electricity and magnetism, forces and motion, light and sound, the earth and beyond and energy resources and energy transfer.

Attainment levels

Whereas the programme of study gives the teacher (and student, for that matter) the entire content that should be taught, the level of difficulty is given by the attainment levels. These range from level 1 through to level 7 or 8 at the end of Key Stage 3. There is a formal assessment at the end of Key Stage 3 (usually in early May of year 9), externally marked, at which the student is given a final level in science. The classroom teacher is also required to give each student a teacher level, which is also sent to the government. This is not official, but is used by the government for statistical purposes. From 2003 the Standard Attainment Tasks

(SATs) will not provide a test to recognise those few students achieving above Level 7 (i.e. 8 or 'Exceptional Performance'), but the teacher assessment can still be awarded at that level if appropriate. Teacher assessment can also provide essential information on students' progress by using 'sub-levels'.

The attainment levels are particularly broad – a student has to make significant progress to achieve the next level up. To achieve a more regular monitoring of progress, sub-levels can be used to ascertain how near students are to reaching their targets. Students should always know their target level and also the level at which they are currently working. The determination of levels is dealt with under assessment (See Chapter 6), and so by knowing their current status, parents and students can be aware of progress in science both on a personal and national basis.

As with all aspects of the National Curriculum, the attainment levels show differentiation in what is expected at the end of each year and also at the end of Key Stage 3. The expected levels are divided into three sections: students making less progress than expected, most students and students making more progress than expected. Each year every state school in the country receives a performance and assessment report (the 'PANDA') on the test results (as well as the other public examination results). The school is compared with others both locally and nationally, and is also graded on the results achieved (taking into account the type of children in the school, their socio/economic background and so on). As a guideline, the expected levels for students at the end of each year at Key Stage 3 are shown in Figure 2.

Year	Students making less progress than expeced	Most pupils	Students making more progress than expected
7	3/4	4/5	6
8	4	5	6/7
9	4/5	6	7/8

Figure 2. Attainments levels during each year of Key Syage 3.

Cognitive Acceleration through Science Education

Known by the acronym 'CASE' this initiative has been around for many years and has been proved to raise achievement not only in science, but also in other areas of the curriculum, such as mathematics and Design Technology (DT). CASE makes use of a set of lessons involving problem solving and thinking skills. To improve thinking, CASE makes use of 'cognitive conflict' – a term used to describe how students make up a rule for a particular relationship, only to find that the rule does not work in all applications. This conflict sets up other possible pathways for a result, thus improving their skills in evaluation and analysis. Many schools use CASE lessons at Key Stage 3, inserting each stand-alone lesson every two weeks or so throughout the science course.

Key Stage 4

At Key Stage 4, the traditional course has been a GCSE Double Award in science for the large majority of students. However, there are other courses in addition to this that we will look at in this section. We will firstly look at a typical GCSE Science (Double Award).

Science: Double Award

This covers the National Curriculum requirements for the majority of students at Key Stage 4. Differentiation is usually provided by the examination board assessing at two different tiers – a higher tier, providing grades A* through to D or E, and a foundation tier providing grades G up to a maximum of C. The grade awarded to the student is doubled (AA, BB, CC etc) to reflect that the science course is worth two 'normal' GCSE subjects. There are two main forms of this course, the co-ordinated approach and the modular approach.

▶ **Co-ordinated Science**. This is taught as the separate subjects of Biology (Sc2), Chemistry (Sc3) and Physics (Sc4). Sc1 (scientific enquiry) is assessed by means of the coursework component of the GCSE. The course is either taught by specialists or as units corresponding to each discipline. Assessment is by a terminal examination in each of the three science subjects, plus a coursework component that is assessed by the teacher. A sample of coursework is sent to the examination board for moderation purposes. Moderation is a process that takes place by an external examiner to ensure that the marking across examination centres is standardised.

▶ **Modular Science**. This course can also be taught in separate subjects but can also be taught as cross-discipline units of work. At the end of each unit there is a module test that contributes a percentage of the final mark. The remainder of the marks are obtained in the same way as the co-ordinated scheme, that is, by terminal examination and coursework. The advantage of a modular scheme is that it enables students who do well in the module tests to be better motivated by good results. However, for those students who do not do so well in the module tests the modular approach can be demotivating because low marks will then count against them, and they will either be forced to accept a lower grade than they would wish, or have to resit the tests at a later date, when they may well have other subjects to revise for. Which scheme is chosen is a matter of choice by the department as a whole, depending on the type of students you have in your school. Larger schools that are able to staff it sometimes offer a choice between the two courses.

Science: Single Award

This course is aimed at the small percentage of students who wish to specialise in other areas (such as modern languages) and thus provides the minimum science education required by law at Key Stage 4. The single award has the same assessment structure as the double award, but the content of the course is less and so it can be taught in less time than the double award. Some schools use the single award as a course for less able students. This is rather unwise, as conceptually the single award course is equal to the double award course and it was never designed as a course for the less able.

Triple Award Science

This course consists of three separate and independent science subjects examined at GCSE. In many schools this course is offered to a minority of students who are academically able and well motivated. In a large proportion of the schools that offer this course no extra time for science is available, and so the students who undertake this course do so in the knowledge that they will have to study at a faster rate, and that they will have to do a large amount of self-supported tasks. The advantages of the triple award are that the student gains an extra GCSE in science in the same time for a double award. If he or she does not do so well in one of the subjects the lower score will not affect the other two subjects, which is not the case in the double or single award, where the scores for the three disciplines plus the coursework are aggregated and the grade awarded on the total mark. The disadvantage is that usually longer (or extra) terminal examinations have to be taken, and the coursework element of the course is more extensive.

GCSE Science (Applied)

This course was introduced to cater for those students who wish to take a more vocational GCSE course rather than the traditional science on offer. It replaced the GNVQ courses on offer at Key Stage 4. Science (Applied) can be a full double award subject with a full grade range from A* through to G at higher and foundation tiers. Where the course differs is in both its subject content and in its assessment.

▶ **Subject content**. The subject content is in units such as 'Developing scientific skills', 'Science for the needs of society' and 'Science at work'. The content matter includes safety in laboratories, first aid, standard procedures and so on; in fact the sort of practical science needed by scientific technicians in industry.

▶ **Assessment** is partly by examination (for one or more of the modules) and partly by a portfolio of work in the laboratory, which is internally assessed and externally moderated by a sample of portfolios much in the same way as the normal double, single or triple award schemes. This course presents an alternative to the traditional courses on offer. In many schools that have adopted this course, less able students who had previously found the traditional approach difficult and, for that matter, irrelevant, have done well.

Other subjects

Some schools run other GCSE courses linked to the science departments. Sometimes these are run as part of the normal curriculum, but it is more likely that they are run as a club, either during lunchtimes or after school hours. Geology is a popular course that links the science department with those in the geography area. Electronics links the DT department with the science department so that resources and teaching can be shared. If a school is fortunate enough to possess a telescope, one examination board offers a GCSE in astronomy. Although it claims that a telescope is not really necessary to do the course, it is a great asset if one is available.

Post-16 education

The government is committed to 'the 14–19 Curriculum'. There may be many changes in the way students are assessed in the next ten years. The ideas proposed may mean that GCSE courses become less important than they are today, as the vast majority of students will be staying on, either at school, or in sixth-form colleges. In science, the main courses are still the traditional A levels, as well as more vocational courses.

A levels

The traditional A level is split into two sections. One half of the work (the A1 or AS) will be studied during the first year of the two-year course culminating in a terminal examination and the second half (the A2) will be examined at the end of the second year. The subject matter is usually split into modules or units, each of which deals with a particular topic. In addition to the terminal examinations, there are usually module tests similar to the modular GCSE course. Practical ability is assessed either by coursework, or by practical examination.

The weighting of marks for a typical three-science A level course might be as follows:

Biology

AS examination (first year)

Unit	Exam (hrs)	Percentage of the total AS mark	Percentage of the total A level mark
1 Core Principles	1	30	15
2 Genes and genetic engineering	1	30	15
3(a) Physiology and transport	1	25	12.5
3(b) Centre-assessed coursework	–	15	7.5

A2 examination (second year)

Unit	Exam (hrs)	Percentage of the total AS mark	Percentage of the total A level mark
4 Energy, control and continuity	1½	–	15
5(a) Environment	1¼	–	7.5
5(b) Centre-assessed coursework	–	–	7.5

Either Unit 6 or Unit 7 or Unit 8
Unit 6 Applied ecology
Unit 7 Microbes and disease
Unit 8 Behaviour and population

Chemistry

AS examination (first year)

Unit	Exam (hrs)	Percentage of the total AS mark	Percentage of the total A level mark
1 Atomic structure, bonding and periodicity	1	30	15
2 Foundation physical and inorganic chemistry	1	30	15
3(a) Introduction to organic chemistry	1	25	12½
3(b) Centre-assessed coursework *or* exam	2 (practical)	15	7½

A2 Examination (second year)

Unit	Exam (hrs)	Percentage of the total A level mark
4 Further physical and organic chemistry	1½	15
5 Thermodynamics and further inorganic chemistry	2	20
6(a) Objective questions	1	10
6(b) Centre-assessed coursework *or* exam	2 (practical)	15

Physics

AS examination (first year)

Unit		Exam (hrs)	Percentage of the total AS mark	Percentage of the total A level mark
1	Particles, radiation and quantum phenomena	1	30	15
2	Mechanics and modular kinetic theory	1	30	15
3	Current electricity and the elastic properties of solids	1	25	12½
Either				
Practical examination		1	15	7½
or				
Coursework			15	7½

A2 examination (second year)

Unit		Exam	Percentage of the total A level mark
4	Waves, fields and nuclear energy	1½	15
5-9	Astrophysics, medical physics, applied physics, turning points in physics, electronics	1¼	10
Either			
Practical examination		1	15
or			
Coursework			15
10	Structured synoptic questions on Modules 1–4 and the common topic, nuclear instability	2	20

The GNVQ

Some schools offer a GNVQ course that is very similar in structure to that offered at GCSE as GCSE Science (Applied). The GNVQ course also extends to post-16 again offers an alternative to the traditional A-level. Units of work reflect the need for science in society and are high in practical content. Although the GNVQ does not base its assessment solely on examinations, it is certainly not an easy option. The portfolio of work needed for assessment is essentially extensive and deep and requires a great deal of dedication and expertise to achieve.

Schemes of work

Within any department the scheme of work is a vital document to refer to regarding what is to be taught and when. Many departments are using the published QCA scheme of work for Key Stage 3. Other departments use a scheme of work provided by the publishers of the text books they use. For example, Hodder Publications have developed a scheme of work that matches closely the QCA scheme, but it adheres to the order and structure of their **Key Stage 3 course Hodder Science**. However, a large number of departments have developed their own schemes at both Key Stages 3 and 4, and post-16. This is to be commended, as schemes of work should be living documents, changing and improving year on year.

Summary

In this chapter we have looked at the National Curriculum at Key Stages 3 and 4, and the curriculum on offer at post-16. We have looked at the meaning of the National Key Stage 3 Strategy and its implications. Finally, it had been emphasised that the department's scheme of work is the essential document to refer to when ensuring that all the topics needed to be taught are covered.

3

Teaching and Learning

One-minute summary – The purpose of a teacher is not just to teach. Unless his or her students learn, then any teaching will be ineffective. The good teacher will tailor the delivery of material in the classroom to ensure that maximum learning takes place. Recent research into how the brain works has led to the acceptance of **accelerated learning** techniques in the classroom. Accelerated learning is an umbrella term for the adoption of varying practical approaches to learning. The Key Stage 3 Strategy for Science makes use of accelerated learning practices in its approach to teaching. There are four main strands to the accelerated learning approach: the study of brain function, theories of human attention, psychology of achievement and optimum performance and intelligence theories.

The accelerated learning cycle

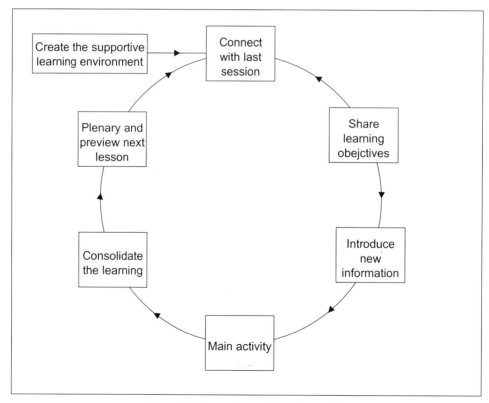

Figure 3. The accelerated learning cycle.

Creating the learning environment

There are many techniques that prepare the student to learn. These include, in no fixed order:

▶ **Relaxation techniques**. These include breathing techniques, stress management and so on. Students will not learn if they are under stress. Disputes with parents or friends, bullying, distractions in the class, physical problems such as poor sight or hearing, and a multitude of other areas can all contribute to stress.

▶ **Team building**. Activities that include every member of the class. A good example is an activity that requires students to find out and share positive qualities about the class members.

▶ **Feedback**. Regular and positive feedback is vital if the student is to have self-esteem regarding the subject. Marking a book as simply '9/10' is not particularly helpful to a student. What he or she needs is to know just *how well* he or she is doing and *how to improve*. A simple formative statement such as 'Good account, but perhaps you need to give more reasons for... to get the next grade up' is much better. This feedback need not be written; it could be given verbally, especially, if your time is precious. In your statement focus on the successes, however small. Use these successes to build on, so that subsequent work incorporates techniques learned previously. Help your students to set modest goals for themselves: 'Next week, Amanda, I would like you to aim for a grade B 5. You can easily achieve this by...'.

▶ **Start and end of lessons**. Simple rituals that anticipate the learning to come or consolidate what has been learned are very useful. A greeting of each student at the door, a simple 'bye' at the end, eye contact, a question about how the team got on last evening, all help contribute to the atmosphere.

▶ **Visual stimuli** around the room – posters are fine though students' own work is much better. Even better are posters made by the students. Posters that show scientific facts or principles such as the differences between metals and non metals, the five main groups of invertebrates (with examples), magnetic fields of bar magnets, etc create an atmosphere that says 'here you will learn about science'. Student's work that consists of pages of neat writing displayed on the wall may give the individual students whose work is displayed some self-esteem, but do little else to stimulate the rest of the class. Lists of key words on the wall aid literacy in science. The pH table (in multicolour), the sodium atom, a typical animal or plant cell, labelled with the correct scientific terms, the path of light through a lens or prism are posters that can be made by students that constantly remind them of key points in the science course. Finally, simple statements around the room also remind the students why they are there. An A3 piece of paper taped to the door with the words 'What did you learn today' is effective. I love the quote of Gene Krantz, the controller of the fated Apollo 13 mission when all around were expecting disaster. He simply stated, 'Failure is not an option!' I have that quote hanging in my room today.

▶ **Consistent expectations**. Some of your students will have quite an unstable background. School may be the only place in their lives that guarantees a level of certainty about how they will be treated. *Consistency* is the rule. If possible, a whole-school approach to this is best, but failing this a well thought-out behaviour policy based on creating and maintaining positive self esteem, understood by all the students and consistently applied is one of the most important factors in the success of accelerated learning. Behaviour management is dealt with in more detail in Chapter 4.

Give an overview

It is very important that the student knows what he or she will have learned (or at least be expected to have learned) by the end of the lesson. Starting the lesson with the phrase 'Today we will be looking at photosynthesis' is nowhere near as effective as 'Today you will be *learning* what *causes* photosynthesis and what a plant *uses* and *produces* when it photosynthesises'. The key objectives can be written on the board in note fashion:

> *What causes photosynthesis?*
> *What does a plant use during photosynthesis?*
> *What does a plant produce during photosynthesis?*

Giving a clear overview of the lesson emphasises what you expect students to have achieved by the end of the lesson. An overview focuses the mind of the student to be clear on what he or she is *expected to achieve* by the end of the lesson.

Connection

Students learn better if they do not tackle something completely new. Research has shown that students grasp topics better if any new concepts connected with previous learning link with the student's current understanding. Giving analogies is another important technique to aid understanding. As a new teacher teaching Brownian motion, (movement in smoke particles due to the random motion of air molecules colliding with them) I noticed in students' accounts that they thought that they had seen air particles moving under the microscope rather than the effect of the particles' motion. The students had clearly misunderstood this difficult concept. Nowadays I use the analogy of an elephant on roller-skates on a soccer field being used instead of a football. The students can easily grasp the idea that the 22 players kicking the poor elephant will send it around the pitch in a random way. I next tell them to imagine going up in a hot air balloon high enough so that they now cannot see the tiny soccer players. What *will* they see? They'll see an elephant, looking like a speck of dust randomly moving about as if by its own accord. Why can't they see the players? The answer is that they are too small. It is an easy matter to translate this silly story to the idea of Brownian motion – the players being the air molecules and the elephant a smoke particle.

Describe the outcome

After the initial overview, the good teacher will explain to his students what they should know or have learned by the end of the lesson. This may not be the same for all the students. In a mixed ability class of students, some may need to achieve far more than others. However, the good teacher should make clear to his or her students just what is expected of each and every one of them. This seems a daunting task, but, as in primary schools, grouping of students by ability within the classroom is not a difficult task.

Each table can be given a different task to perform or even a different worksheet with different outcomes. In the photosynthesis lesson table one (special needs students) may be asked to find out the simple answers to the three objectives in the overview – the answers 'light', 'carbon dioxide and water' and 'sugar and oxygen' may be sufficient. However, with table seven (gifted and talented students), they would be expected to find out the same answers as table one, but with extra details such as the type of light involved (does green light have an effect?), the concentration of carbon dioxide, the type of sugar produced and so on. In describing the outcome in this way, *all* students will feel involved.

Another method is to share the investigation of several variables around the room. Investigation of the variables that affect the bounce of a squash ball can be shared so that the easy-to-measure variables (such as type of ball, height dropped, etc.) are investigated by some students, whereas the more difficult variables (squashability, surface texture on which it is dropped, etc.) can be tackled by other, more able students. At the end of the lesson, however, all the results will count towards the initial objective of finding out what affects the bounce of a squash ball so that all students feel that their results have contributed to the final answers.

Questions and answers

A question and answer session prior to the main lesson activity not only ensures that the students are geared up to learn. It is an excellent assessment tool for the skilful teacher. The type of question asked, however, needs to be open-ended and searching. One of the faults of inexperienced teachers is to ask questions that require a 'yes' or 'no' answer to those students with their hands up. In this scenario, the most able are not stretched, those who have an opinion are not allowed, by the nature of the question, to express it and it is too easy for some students to slip into the background of the class unnoticed. Also, it is important to invite answers from an equal mixture of boys and girls.

Another fault is to expect an answer too quickly. A good idea is to say, before posing the question, that you wish the students to think about the answer before putting up their hands. This 'thinking time' could be anything between 10 and 20 seconds. Invite a response from a student when at least half the class has their hands up.

What about the student who never puts up his hand? It is a little daunting for the student to be questioned directly, but an effective method is to include him gently in the conversation by asking his or her opinion on a previously answered question. For example a question might be posed regarding the cause of conduction in solids. You pose the question 'Suggest some causes why the heat travels along the metal bar?' You wait for 'thinking time' and invite responses and list the possibilities on the board. One response might be totally wrong, at which point you can invite the student who is never forthcoming to suggest whether he or she agrees with that response and, if possible, say why. In this way, you achieve your expectation of involving every student without putting any of them on the spot which will only make him or her even less likely to respond in the future.

Activity

The nature of the activity or activities is as varied as the topic matter being studied. Organising practical sessions, group work and demonstrations are dealt with in Chapters 5 and 7. However, the activities should be varied so that all the students achieve their potential. The use of multiple intelligence information (see below) and differentiation will effectively enhance learning.

Review

At the end of the activity the students will have collected together evidence, results or information and should be reaching conclusions that mirror the original lesson objectives. The review session is the most important part of the lesson for it is within that time that *most of the lesson's learning takes place*. The review session, to be effective, should take at least 15 minutes – which for many schools is around 25% of the lesson time. You can split the review session into three distinct areas:

▶ Further question and answer session for the students to consolidate their conclusions.

▶ Review of the lesson objectives to reiterate what they should have learned.

▶ A simple exercise for the students themselves to review what they have learned.

The question and answer session needs to be structured so that the students can consolidate what they have learned. The questions need to follow quite closely the objectives that you laid down at the start of the lesson and the knowledge/ understanding/skills that you expected all the students to learn. In addition to the bulk of the questions, a few may be used at the end to consolidate those areas that only the most able will have experienced or learned.

The review of the lesson objectives can be tackled in a number of ways. One easy way is to ask the students to copy down the key points that they have learned as a summary. With only a few statements even special needs students will be able to manage this.

Finally, the students themselves need to have realised that they have learned something in the lesson. One way is to simply ask them to write down five things that they have learned in the lesson that they did not know before. Ask them to compare their list with that of the student next to them to arrive at a common list of five or more items. Each pair can then combine with another pair to form a small group and repeat the exercise. At the end ask a spokesperson from each group to read out a selection and write them on the board. In this way, all students are involved in the learning experience and the key points are revisited several times.

The key to a good lesson is simply:

▶ Tell them what they *will* learn.
▶ Tell them what they *are* learning.
▶ Tell them what they *have* learned.
▶ Tell them what they have learned *again. . .and again.*

Preview what's next

Many a lesson has ended with the review session. It is however important that students also see the context into which an individual lesson fits. A simple statement such as 'Today we have learned today the main effects of an electrical current – heating, electromagnetic and chemical. Next lesson we shall be concentrating on just one of these – the heating effect – and learn more about it'.

Other aspects of teaching and learning

Differentiation

Differentiation involves tailoring the teaching practices and environments to create learning experiences appropriate to the needs of different students. In many science departments cohorts of students are set by ability and so a relatively narrow band of ability lies within each set. Appropriate work can therefore be broadly differentiated across a cohort by this means. However, within a class there will be a band of ability and needs, even in a setted situation, and these needs should also be addressed through differentiation. Maker's model of differentiation in the classroom (Maker, 1982a 1982b, 1986) suggests that there are four main areas where differentiation should be achieved:

1. The Learning Environment.

The type of tasks set the students should focus on the *students' interests* and *ideas* rather than those of the teacher. A good example of this in the science context is the setting of open-ended practical investigations, where differentiation results from the depth at which the investigation takes place. This is known as 'differentiation by outcome'. Students should be encouraged to:

▶ undertake independent research;

▶ evaluate others' opinions and ideas;

▶ use a wide range of resources such as the Internet, books and CD-ROMs;

▶ use a range of media for recording and reporting results either in the form of:
  – a written report
  – a presentation to the class using overhead transparencies or Powerpoint, or
  – the production of a video.

Students should also be encouraged to work as part of a team, either in the classroom, the laboratory, the library resource centre or even out of school, perhaps involving other schools, local businesses or other external agencies.

2. Modifying the content of the syllabus

The idea is to remove the ceiling on what is learned. Naturally, with a less able group, the syllabus content needs to be at the correct level so that the students undertake topics in line with their ability. However, whatever the ability of the child, the aim is to encourage the acquisition of a knowledge base by utilising a more diverse learning experience. This may be achieved by the teaching of concepts, relationships and generalisation rather than facts and descriptions in isolation. Students need to learn the interrelation between ideas rather than the isolated ideas themselves. An example of this would be in the teaching of periodicity. Teaching atomic structure and periodicity in isolation means that patterns that link the two ideas are lost. It is much better to look for patterns and relationships in both topics, than studying each as if they were completely separate. Finally, it is important to expand on the material that would normally be taught in the unit of work, time permitting, if students are to be stretched and challenged.

3. Modifying the process of learning
In a class of students there will be many who will find, for the main activity, a worksheet, sufficient instruction. Others will need a worksheet plus verbal teacher input. Others may need the continual input of a learning support assistant if there is to be any real learning. The skilful teacher, knowing his or her students, will have allowed for this by giving alternative approaches to the activity. A simple way is to produce two worksheets – one with a normal font (say Times New Roman) and another using a sanserif font such as Arial. The difference that a larger, simpler font will make to the readability of the worksheet is quite remarkable. Worksheets for less able students should have more pictorial or diagrammatic ways of giving instructions. Make sure, however, that the worksheet diagrams show the same equipment that you or your technician has provided. As for written activities, a prose method will be fine for more able students but for those with learning difficulties simple writing frames or incomplete sentences (with jumbled words provided underneath) are more effective. Avoid simply copying from the board – all students need to show some evidence of brain process whether it is an original piece of prose, the use of writing frames or the completion of simple sentences, in order that learning is effective.

4. Modifying the product of learning
It is quite possible to set the same activity or project for all the students in a class irrespective of their ability. I have used open-ended project work and find it an effective way of learning. Moreover, the students *like* research based project work, and if the Internet is used as a tool in this way, many cross-curricular skills can be obtained as a bonus. A project on, say, 'metals' needs to be qualified with what you, as the teacher, expect the students to find out. For example, the students could research how metals were originally discovered (linking in, for the more able, to why gold and silver were known to the ancients because of their lack of reactivity and hence why they are found native), how they are obtained from ores, their physical properties, their chemical properties, their uses and so on. The most able students will cover all these aspects and more for a variety of metals – the less able will possibly research just one or two in less depth. Thus students, working at their own level, will end up with a product reflecting their ability, and so differentiation by outcome will be the result. It is, however, important that you, knowing the students, will ensure that the able student has produced work befitting his or her ability! A good ending to the project is to arrange for each student or group of students to give a talk to the rest of the class on an aspect of their work. It does wonders for the self-esteem of less able students if they are able to give such a talk to the rest of the class – and even more so if they are able to demonstrate deeper knowledge of a particular topic than those that are traditionally thought of as 'better at science' in the class by answering questions put to them by their friends.

Literacy and numeracy

Literacy in science can be tackled in many ways. As well as the normal experimental accounts, simple word games, crosswords and even wordsearches help to consolidate key words and their spelling within the science context. In every classroom or laboratory there should be, on display, a list above head height, of the main key words used in science. The use of spider diagrams, note-taking, skimming information and the uses of précis are all key skills needed for good examination revision. Often these skills have to be taught and so the good science teacher will liaise with the literacy co-ordinator to find the best way in which these skills can be used in the science context. Science is a numerate subject, especially at Key Stage 4. However, if numeracy is to be taught within the science curriculum, it is essential that liaison between the mathematics department and the science department ensures that the method behind calculations is consistent to avoid confusion.

Gifted and talented students

Gifted and talented students make up the top few per cent of the student population. However, exceptionally able pupils do not always display academic excellence. Some may even display behavioural problems. Some may be seen as successful at school, but like those students whose true ability may not be recognised, they may not achieve their potential in the classroom. Those students, who are deemed gifted need to be challenged, developed and extended. More of the same is a poor substitute. An open-ended challenging task is necessary if the gifted child is to achieve the level of work of which he or she is capable. The good teacher will not only show differentiation in the classroom or laboratory – there should be tasks that only the most able will master.

For example, take the effect of various factors on the rate of a chemical reaction, a standard investigation at the end of Key Stage 3 or at the start of Key Stage 4. The effect of the variables, concentration and temperature is investigated using the reaction of sodium thiosulphate with dilute hydrochloric acid to produce colloidal sulphur. The student looks down through the flask onto a tile on which is drawn a cross. When the cross disappears the reaction time is recorded. The reaction is performed at different concentrations of thiosulphate and temperatures.

When drawing a conclusion for the effect of concentration the lowest level of inference might be:

'If the solution is concentrated the reaction is fast – if it is diluted it is slow.'

A higher level response is:

'As the concentration gets higher, the reaction gets faster.'

A response requiring higher conceptual thinking might be:

'As the concentration gets higher, the reaction gets faster in proportion.'

(i.e. one is directly proportional to the other). The last response would only be given by more able students doing the same activity.

However, for the *most* able, a further investigation could be possible. As well as simply drawing the graph of the concentration against the time to get a curve (indicating some form of relationship) the gifted child could be asked to research the *nature* of the relationship. *Is* the relationship one of *direct* or *inverse* proportion? To achieve this a reciprocal plot is needed – of the concentration against 1/time. In an inversely proportional relationship, the reciprocal plot is a straight line through the origin. In the case of the above reaction, the relationship between the concentration and the time *is* inversely proportional, but that between the temperature and time is not. As an open-ended task, the gifted child could then be asked to use the Internet to do some research to find out:

(a)   why one is proportional but the other is not

(b)   what actually *is* the nature of the relationship.

In this way, the child is continuing to complete the work of the rest of the class, but is also being challenged to work at a much higher conceptual level.

Multiple intelligences

In 1983 Dr Howard Gardner, professor of education at Harvard University, suggested that the idea of intelligence based on IQ only was far too limited, and so eight different types of intelligence were proposed to account for a much broader range of potential. In schools where multiple intelligence data is used effectively in teaching there has been a marked raising of achievement especially in those students where the traditional ideas of intelligence (namely verbal and mathematical) are not developed as fully as others. The eight types of intelligence are:

▶ **Linguistic intelligence (Li)** – students have a good verbal ability and can be referred to as 'word smart'. They are good at word games, anagrams, and general literacy.

▶ **Logical and mathematical intelligence (Lo)** – students have a good grasp of number concept and are good at solving logical problems.

▶ **Spatial intelligence (Sp)** – known as 'picture smart' – these students envisage concepts in pictures and diagrams. When revising they are more likely to produce spider-diagrams or mind maps.

▶ **Musical intelligence (Mu)** – students exhibiting this form of intelligence, either as melody or rhythm do well in musical activities and would find remembering facts much more easy if set to a song or rap.

▶ **Intrapersonal intelligence (Ip)** – students are likely to reflect on themselves, and might learn best on their own, using self-supported study packs.

▶ **Bodily-kinaesthetic intelligence (Bk)** – as the name implies, these students learn best through movement and physical experiences. The student who is disaffected in the classroom, but who is outstanding on the football field, is a classic example.

▶ **Interpersonal intelligence (Ia)** – refers to the student who works best through interaction with others, and who does well in activities such as group work.

▶ **Naturalistic intelligence (Na)** – students possessing this form of intelligence learn best through interaction with and experience of the natural world.

The predominant intelligence or intelligences are tested for using a simple questionnaire available from *http://www.ldpride.net/learningstyles.MI.htm*. Many schools test students as they arrive at the school along with Cognitive Ability Tests and Edinburgh reading tests so that this data and SATs results can be used effectively in raising achievement by realistic target setting and level/grade prediction.

Everyone possesses all these forms of intelligence in differing amounts. However, it is useful to the teacher to use the most dominant form in their lesson preparation, and therefore to be aware that there are students in their classes that have these differing abilities. It is impossible to provide all eight approaches in each lesson, nor would that be desirable. However, armed with the information about their students, science teachers can incorporate some of the approaches into their lessons so that students can have at least some of the lesson delivered in their preferred style.

For example, suppose that you are doing a lesson on the effect of light intensity on photosynthesis. A worksheet could be produced with written instructions (Li) together with diagrams (Sp). What to measure (Lo) and record, and the effect on the plants or type of plants needed (Na) could be discussed. The students are then put into groups and an investigation performed (Ia). Controlled movement around the class, for example to collect equipment, put results on a computer spreadsheet and so on, is desirable to help those with bodily-kinaesthetic intelligence (Bk). In the plenary session students can be asked to write down, without anyone watching, three things they have learned in the lesson (Ip). Finally, as homework, the students are asked to set the three facts to a jingle, either a well-known song or one they made up, to aid remembering the facts (Mu). Thus in the space of one lesson all the intelligence types could be included, but naturally this is not going to happen day by day. However, it is important that the teacher is aware of the types and the positive effect that this can have on student achievement.

Emotional intelligence

The psychologist Daniel Goleman once defined emotional intelligence as 'the ability to monitor one's own and others' emotions, to discriminate among them, and to use the information to guide one's thinking and actions'. The theory surrounding emotional intelligence is that it exists as a separate form of intelligence apart from that traditionally accepted by schools. It is important that these students should be recognised as intelligent, in their own unique way, and helped to develop their special skills so that they too have the opportunity to be successful in this society. They need to believe (as should their parents and teachers) that these abilities are equally important and as highly regarded as traditional intelligence. Emotional intelligence can be assessed, as can multiple intelligence, by questionnaire, and lessons adapted, where possible, to accommodate this.

In many schools the majority of students come from stable backgrounds where there is a great deal of parental support both in quality time spent with their offspring and also financially (e.g. providing resources such as Internet access, books and a quiet place to study). However, in some cases students have little support in the home, or come from poorer families where the resourcing of education is not of as much importance as the need to provide food, clothing and shelter on a limited budget. In this latter case, emotional intelligence usually gives a much better indication of future performance than cognitive assessment or reading tests, as emotional intelligence takes into account the general motivation of the student, as well as his or her innate intelligence.

Summary

Education is about teaching but equally about learning. The successful teacher will take seriously the way in which all of his or her students learn and tailor lessons and the way in which he or she teaches to maximise that learning.

4

Discipline

One-minute summary – Although some learning can take place in the classroom even with mediocre teaching, little, if any learning will take place unless there is good discipline in the class. Good classroom management is not something that you either have or do not have, although it may be true to say that it usually improves with experience; it is a skill that can be learned like any other, if you put into practice some ground rules. In this chapter we will be dealing with a few basic principles, and expanding on those that have most effect. Therefore, to ensure good discipline in the classroom, these principles will be an excellent starting point. The principles laid down in this chapter come under the umbrella term of 'assertive discipline'. The name most associated with assertive discipline is Lee Canter in the USA, who has written a great deal on the subject. Assertive discipline is a structured, systematic approach designed to assist teachers in running an organised, teacher-in-charge classroom environment. It is not without its critics, but for the newly qualified teacher assertive discipline's basic principles make an excellent starting point.

The classroom discipline plan

Before you can expect students to behave in a classroom, you first need to decide what you will expect of them, how you will reward them if they are doing well, and what punishments you will make use of if there is a discipline problem. A statement of these parameters is called a classroom discipline plan. You should make up your own plan using the guidelines here and publish this to your students. It is always in three sections: expectations, rewards and sanctions.

Expectations

Expect the highest standards, both in behaviour and quality of work and *insist on them*. One of the basic errors in classroom discipline is that the teacher assumes that the students know innately how to behave. More often than not the students will not know exactly what is expected of them, so they will need to be told. Students who know exactly where they stand with a teacher are often less likely to be a disruptive influence in the classroom. One of the first things any new teacher should do is to make a 'classroom discipline plan' on A3 paper and display it in a prominent place in the laboratory. An A5 version could be copied for students to put in their books. The first part of the plan should consist of your **expectations**, and should consist of no more than three or four points so that they are easily committed to memory. A typical list of expectations might be as follows:

Expectations
(a) Follow all the teacher's instructions.
(b) Treat others in the class with respect.
(c) Abide by all the laboratory safety rules.

(a) Follow all the teacher's instructions
This is an important part of the discipline plan, as it is a 'catch all' for any situation where there is a possible conflict. The first instruction that should be given to any class is that when you are talking to the class either in classroom discussions, in the plenary session or in any other situation that you designate, the class should be *silent and listening*. Another instruction should be that students should raise their hands to answer questions and should volunteer an answer only at your invitation.

(b) Treat others in the class with respect
Many conflicts in the classroom are not a reaction against the subject, the teacher or the 'establishment', but are a direct result of squabbles that have occurred before your lesson and which are now being brought into the classroom. It is important that you **insist** that students leave any 'baggage' outside the classroom, and that they treat each other with respect. In turn you should set an example by treating the students with respect by the way you speak and act. As a professional you should set an example to the students.

(c) Abide by all the laboratory safety rules
This is vital during practical sessions. Although this expectation could be included under the umbrella of 'Following instructions', by making it a separate expectation, you are drawing attention to the importance of safety in the room both for the sake of the students and for your own safety.

Rewards
Nothing improves motivation more than praise. Even disaffected students usually thrive on praise. If a student is succeeding then they are more likely to enjoy the subject, work harder and achieve even more. Therefore, behaviour can be a spiral *upwards* but equally *downwards* if the wrong approach is made. Rewards play a large part in the upward spiral. Again, as with expectations, rewards need to be shared with and understood by the whole class. A typical set of rewards written below your expectations on your classroom discipline plan might be:

Rewards
(a) Verbal praise.
(b) House points.
(c) Commendation.
(d) Homework pass.
(e) Whole class reward.

(a) Verbal praise
A simple 'well done', a thumbs up sign or similar gesture to show that you are pleased with what the student has done, or is doing, is an indication to the student that he or she is succeeding, and is likely to be motivating. If a class is working well with the exception of a couple of students who are not on task, then it is often sufficient to praise the others individually around the students that are off-task. Wanting praise themselves they will usually get the message and knuckle down to work. However, when giving verbal praise, try to give at least three praise comments for each negative comment. If there is a student, or students, in a class who are disruptive, try very hard to praise them when they do something, however small, to your liking. In this way they will gradually be conditioned into conforming to your expectations.

(b) Merit system
Many schools operate a house point or merit system that leads to a reward of a certificate or prize when the student reaches 10, 25, 50 or 100 merits as well as earning points (and therefore 'street-cred') for their house or tutor group/form group. Students are much more motivated to positively engage in these systems when they know exactly how to get a house point or a merit. For example achieving an 'A' in their homework, answering a particularly difficult question in class, drawing a difficult diagram well – all may be worthy of house points or merits. One other way to motivate students is to give out a cloakroom ticket every time they get a house point or merit. When a certain number have been allocated in a class, say 100, have a raffle. Draw one of the stubs from a box – whoever wins gets the prize of a large bar of chocolate or something similar. As a head of department I would always put aside a small sum of money from capitation (or bid acquisition) as a prize fund from which items like this can be purchased. The good thing about this system is that those students who receive the most house points or merits are more likely to receive the prize because more stubs bearing their name will be in the box. What about the others, though, the losers? If you pre-arrange the number of house points or merits, say 100, that have to be obtained before this raffle, this can also be the number that has to be received in order to get a whole class reward (see below). Therefore, even though most of the class did not win the prize, it is important that everyone feels they have contributed to the class reward, even if they have managed just one house point or merit.

(c) Commendation
Sometimes, especially with older children, a written commendation signed by you or the head of department is more motivating. Even simpler is a quick telephone call to the student's parents. Too often the only time parents receive such calls is when there is a problem and so they will usually be very pleased and reward their child again at home.

(d) Homework pass

If you wish to reward excellent behaviour and work, a homework pass is often motivating. Providing that such a pass is not against departmental or school policy, it indicates to the student that, for that week they are someone special, and that you are so pleased with them they are able to have more time free instead of doing extra science homework. With this kind of reward, it can only be used for a student a maximum of once or twice a term, or they may end up falling behind with their work. Also, a standard letter should accompany the child home to commend the child and to explain to the parents why their child will not have homework that evening. This commendation will be motivating in itself, but the need not to do homework will be doubly so.

(e) Whole class reward

When a class reaches a preset number of house/merit points, you can offer the class a reward. This could be a week off homework, a trip, or a video at the end of term instead of a lesson. Whatever the reward, the golden rule is that it must be their choice. What might be a reward to you may be an ordeal to a teenager! I had one class some time ago where, as a whole class reward they wanted a trip to Wookey Hole in Somerset. I explained that it would be possible, but they would have to fund it themselves, as it would be expensive. They decided as a group to give up crisps and sweets from the tuck shop for a few weeks, and save the money towards the trip. The group contained some of the school's least able students, many from poor backgrounds. Such was their motivation that we had an excellent day out, with no trouble.

3. Sanctions

However well-motivated the majority of your students will be there will always be some that will need to be disciplined by using some form of sanction. As with the previous two sections it is vital for good classroom control that the students know exactly where they stand with regard to punishment. The golden rule here is **consistency**. Also, if you threaten to carry out a punishment it *has* to be carried out or you will be seen as weak. The scale of the punishment is of little relevance, as long as it is seen to be carried out whenever there is a breach of your classroom discipline plan. Incidentally, it is more effective and less threatening to students if you make it clear that it is their *behaviour* not them *personally* that you will not accept. A typical plan as far as sanctions is concerned is given below. Note that the plan should not have more sanctions than rewards – keep things positive! This should be added to your plan after your expectations and your rewards:

Sanctions
(a) Warning (stage 1).
(b) Move to another place (stage 2).
(c) Keep in after the lesson for 3–5 minutes depending upon the misdemeanour (stage 3)

(d) Science detention (stage 4)
(e) Referral to senior staff (stage 5).

(a) Warning

If there is an initial breach of your expectations, it is always fair to give a warning: 'This is your only warning – if you choose not to get on with your work, you will move to stage 2 and you will move to sit on your own over there'. Always use the term ' if you *choose* to do/not do. . .). In this way, if a student persists in disrupting a lesson, then he has no one to blame but him or herself if he or she moves on to the next stage. Always give *them* the choice. If you dish out punishments all over the class for misdemeanours, it is not always evident to the student that it is his or her actions that have caused the punishment. This leads to resentment and a breakdown in the relationship between a teacher and his or her class. Don't forget, we have to teach students how to behave in a way that matches our expectations. If, on the other hand, you give them the stark choice – 'If you *choose* to do that then *this* will happen' there will be no one to vent his or her anger on but him or herself. Occasionally students will try to blame others for what they are doing: 'It's not me – *he's* annoying me' is a frequent response. Your response should be firm, showing that you have heard his complaint, but that you insist that he gets on with what he should be doing:

'I understand that, but you need to do this now. . .'.

Do not get into a three-way argument with other students. Another scenario might need you to give more than one warning – up to a maximum of three before moving onto stage 2:

Teacher: 'James, you have work to do. Get away from that window and sit in your seat.'
Student: 'But I want to see what that guy is doing over the road.'
Teacher: 'I understand, but I want you to sit down now.'
Student: 'Just a minute, OK?'
Teacher: 'No, James, I want you to sit down now.'
Student: 'Aw, OK.'

In this scenario, the student has been 'heard' by the teacher, no stressful anger was involved, but all the time the teacher was calm, assertive and got a result. If, however, James had refused again to move, then he would have automatically got to stage 2. Another tactic is not to shout if reprimanding a student. Close proximity works much better – even crouching down to their level, and reiterating your request in a calm, but assertive, way. Also, if they are *not* doing what you expect, you should always tell them *what* to do. Often students go off-task because they simply do not know what to do or how to do it. An example of this might be:

Teacher: 'Jane, you have that exercise to do. Stop annoying Paul.'

Jane: 'But he started it Miss. . .'

Teacher: 'I understand Jane but you need to get exercises 2 and 3 completed'.

Jane: 'But he *started* it . . .'

Teacher: 'Yes Jane, I heard you and I understand. . . But you still need to get started on Exercises 2 and 3 *now*.'

By showing empathy with Jane in understanding that it was not her fault originally (but also not overtly blaming Paul) you can then insist that your original request be carried out. Do not forget: Unless there is a biological problem, ***there is no acceptable reason for any misbehaviour in a class.***

(b) Move to another place

This sanction is at stage 2 in our model discipline plan. Moving to another place means that the student is not able to sit with his or her friends. Being isolated either outside the classroom or inside it is something that students simply do not like. However, to be effective, you should isolate them for a short time and then give them the choice of returning to get on with their work. Do not forget that it is *their* choice. If they choose to return, then it will be under *your* terms, in that you expect them to get on with their work without interruption. If they subsequently choose not to do this then they need to be told that they will immediately move on to stage 3. Be clear in what you expect, and be clear in what will be the consequences if they choose not to abide by your discipline plan. If they choose not to return, then make sure that, in isolation, they carry on with their work. You might, however, point out to them that you are disappointed that they lack so much self-discipline that they cannot get on with their tasks without being isolated from their peers. Do not forget, however, that they should be praised if they get on with their work during the remainder of the lesson – positive reinforcement is a good tool in order to motivate children.

(c) Keep in after the lesson for 3–5 minutes depending upon the misdemeanour

Do not forget that the length of time that a child is detained is of little consequence. Keeping a child in at the end of the lesson for just *two* minutes means a great deal. It means that he or she does not know where the rest of their friends have gone and so may lose out socially during break time. They will not get to the front of the Tuck Shop queue. The best places in the playground or on the field, for playing a game, will have been taken by others. As stage 3 in the plan, two or three minutes reprimand from you – isolated from their peers – is not pleasant for a student and it is something that he or she will not want to happen often. It is also important to add that reprimands of this sort should be carried out *in private*. If a reprimand is necessary during a lesson always invite the student into the corridor so that they are not embarrassed in front of their peers. Adolescents respect their privacy more than anything else, and a public put-down might make *you* feel a little better, but it will build up resentment in the student, and create a situation where a small discipline matter might become more serious later on.

(d) Science detention

All good science departments will have a disciplinary set-up that will usually have some sort of detention system run by the head of department. Should a student have reached stage 4 in our plan, then there is no alternative but to arrange for a detention. This will mean that a letter will get sent home to his or her parents and the student kept in to do extra work. There is nothing wrong with the newly qualified teacher doing the detention himself, neither is there anything wrong in involving your head or department. Teachers who involve senior staff are not seen as 'weak' by the students. In fact, the involvement of senior staff means that to a student the department is unified and acting as a team. If a student sees that you actually communicate, he or she will be less likely to play one member of staff off against another.

(e) Referral to senior staff

Unfortunately, in any school there will be some students that will pass through the systems in place and, for varying reasons, will find themselves disrupting lesson after lesson. As a newly qualified teacher, having gone through your plan, if the student continues to disrupt, then you will have to involve senior staff in the school. Some schools operate a '999' or 'red card' system where senior staff are on duty and will come into your class and remove offending youngsters. Other schools operate a referral unit to which students are sent. Whatever the set-up in your particular school, you will need to find out how it works and stick to the rules. If slips need to be filled in or forms completed stating the problem, it is important that these are done. For one thing, the form tutor and year head or house leader needs to know what has happened, and, if there are major problems with the youngster, these slips will need to be produced as evidence, if the child is to be excluded from school.

Ten tips for success

Having now looked at assertive discipline in the classroom, there are ten simple tips that, if you commit to memory, should stand you in good stead in any classroom. Do not forget that good classroom discipline and management can and *must* be learned. Do not believe the person who says he or she never has problems in the classroom – we all will in our careers. It is how we deal with them that matters.

Tip 1. Think about your approach in the classroom
Think about the strategies you plan to use to encourage positive classroom

behaviour. Knowing your own expectations will make it easier for you to lead the class confidently and effectively. Humour, appropriately used, helps create a good atmosphere, as does a pleasant, courteous and calm approach.

Tip 2. Be prepared for any situation
Imagine possible classroom conflicts and develop in your mind your strategies for dealing with them. Having clear-cut strategies will help when (sadly, not 'if'!) these challenges arise.

Tip 3. Make your expectations clear
Make sure that students know what you expect of them.

Tip 4. Model positive behaviour
Occasionally, you may have to remind yourself to follow your own rules. For example, if you ask students not to drink in the laboratory, don't keep a cup of coffee on your desk.

Tip 5. Praise, praise and praise again
When you praise students who are excelling, don't forget to encourage those who are trying, but struggling.

Tip 6. Show respect to your students
This includes listening to their needs and preserving their dignity. It also means living up to their expectations of you, such as greeting them at the beginning of class and returning homework marked and on time.

Tip 7. Keep students busy and challenged
Busy students, working at an appropriate level, are far less likely to exhibit disruptive behaviour.

Tip 8. Make the rules challenging
Create a classroom where the rules are easily followed but challenging to the students. Try to lay down rules of respect and positive behaviour that lasts.

Tip 9. Make sure that the students know the sanctions you will use
You should spell out what will happen if students do not meet your expectations.

Finally – the most important tip of all!

Tip 10. Be consistent
Be sure to address your students' behaviour in a consistent manner. Be wary of moving the goalposts when misbehaviour occurs. To students, this will show a lack of decisiveness and weakness. Find the classroom discipline plan you like *and stick with it.*

Summary

In this chapter we have looked at the basic principles of assertive discipline within the classroom. The classroom discipline plan consists of three sections, expectations, rewards and sanctions. However, if one word is used to sum up good discipline in the class room it would be consistency – consistency in what you expect, so the students know your standards; consistency in your rewards, so that you cannot be accused of favouritism or 'picking on' anyone, and consistency in the use of sanctions so that the students know that you will and do punish every time if they choose not to meet your standard.

5

A Good Science Lesson

One-minute summary – As a trainee teacher, or one who is newly qualified, you will be regularly observed in the classroom. Not only your teaching will be assessed but also how well the students learn. This process does not end, however, after your induction year. In any good school there will be processes in place that enable you to observe and be observed as part of professional development and performance management so that, given enough experience, you will be competent to progress through the upper pay spine threshold and progress through the profession. As someone who has observed many lessons, taken by student teachers, newly qualified staff and by more experienced colleagues, the standard of teaching and learning, though varying to some degree, has never been higher. Part of this success is due to the focus of many schools on success and achievement, and the means to obtain it. The Key Stage 3 National Strategy has advocated the 'three-part-lesson', but in reality science teachers have been doing this for many years. I know, I was introduced to this when I was trained in the 1970s. By now we should be experts! However, initiatives aside, it cannot be stressed enough that an effective science lesson must have a tight structure and very clear objectives. Good science lessons are most effective when the students in the class are themselves clear about what is expected of them, both in the subject matter and in classroom discipline. Good lessons are only good as a result of careful planning by the teacher, taking into account such things as the ability of the children, the subject matter, differentiation, preferred learning styles and even the time of the day.

In this chapter we will be looking more closely at a typical three-part generic lesson. Naturally, not all lessons will fall into a three-part format – for example, some may involve a test, others revision questions and so on. Nevertheless, the main bulk of teaching and learning should take place in a three-part structure to be as effective as possible. The golden rule for three-part lessons is simple:

1. Tell the students what they will do.
2. Tell the students what they are doing.
3. Tell the students what they have done.

A typical science lesson can vary depending on the type of work that pupils are to do. A practical lesson, and particularly those that involve scientific enquiry of an extended nature, will require different planning and management from lessons that are focused on the reinforcement of knowledge and understanding. The 'three part lesson' in this case may well extend over two or more lessons. However, the three parts should be there nevertheless.

Before the lesson

(a) You will need to know the type of students in the class. What is the ability of the class as a whole (set 1, 2, 3, mixed ability etc)? Are there any statemented students in the class? Any who are gifted and talented? What are their preferred learning styles? Good schools will give you, along with set lists, a package of data for each student such as various types of IQ score, reading test scores, target levels or grades, preferred learning styles, emotional quotient, previous SATs scores and so on. Based on the information you have researched you should know the general profile of the class, and the level at which you should pitch the lesson.

(b) Work out your objectives for the lesson. What do you require the students to learn? Are there any terms that you need them to understand? Try to concentrate on three key points that you need to get across. This will be your lesson focus.

(c) If you intend to provide a worksheet, then you will need to ensure that it is at an appropriate reading age for the students to cope with. Students who are less able will need more diagrams and less text. Sentence construction needs to be simple, with possibly one simple idea per sentence. The font you use is of great importance – elaborate fonts confuse poor readers. Much better is a sanserif font such as Arial, News Gothic or Gautami. The point size should be at least 12, 13 or 14. Do not use colour, as this obviously will not photocopy cheaply. For less able groups, try to include some literacy-based activity, such as the solving of anagrams of the key words that you wish them to learn. Also ensure, for all groups, that you have made clear on the sheet what you expect them all to do, and what you expect some of them to do. By differentiating a worksheet in this way, you will keep those quicker learners productive, thus keeping possible disruption to a minimum. Make sure that the worksheet is completed to allow for reprographic time.

(d) Next you will need to look at resources for the lesson. Technicians are, in the main, amazingly willing to accommodate late booking of equipment, but try not to abuse their good nature. Good practice is to sit down with your technician weekly and to plan the next week's resources so that he or she can start preparing lessons for you straight away. There will also be sufficient time to change things if there is a clash over apparatus.

(e) Before the class arrives, it is good practice to write on the board the lesson objectives. Rather than just stating them it is clearer for the pupils to have the lesson objectives shared in this way:

1.   By the end of the lesson you will learn that...
2.   By the end of the lesson you will be able to...
3.   By the end of the lesson you will know that...

Naturally, all the lesson objectives might be in the style of one of the above. In this way, the students have a clear idea if what is expected of them, what they are expected to learn, and have an immediate idea if they have been successful – '*Have* I learned that. . .' It is also a good idea to tape on the door as they leave a card with the message: '*What* did you learn today?' Try, also, to make sure that your classroom or laboratory is stimulating. Posters that may look glossy and which cost a fortune are not necessarily as effective as simply putting a complete list of key words around the room – something that can be done easily at little cost. Try to place the words above head height. Research has shown that posters higher than head height are more effective than those around the middle of the room.

The start of the lesson

Stand at the classroom door ready to greet the students as they come in. If you know their names already, greet them by name as they enter. Set a calm atmosphere. If you do not know their names, learn them quickly. A seating plan (constructed from the set lists) helps. Depending upon the policy of the school (or department), the students should either stand by their places waiting for the invitation to sit, or sit down quietly, getting their equipment out ready to start. If it is the first time that you see the class, and they enter noisily, you should make clear your expectations when going through your discipline plan (see Chapter 4). At this point you may need to go over your expectations on discipline using your plan. Next, any administration (registration, giving out homework) should be done to get it out of the way, leaving the rest of the lesson available to concentrate on the learning. The whole of the settling down period, administration and so on should take no more than five minutes from a one-hour lesson.

Part 1 of the lesson – the introduction

Start the lesson with clear objectives – referring to the list you have written on the board. The first part of the lesson will be the introduction. Go over the objectives with the students using clear language:

'What I am looking for is pupils who can...'
'What I want *all* of you to learn today is. . . *Some* of you will also learn. . .'

There should be a time during the introduction, either before the objectives or after (whichever is appropriate) where there is a review of prior work. This can be done in a number of ways. Here are three examples – but you may have your own ideas.

Questions and answers

It is important not to give too many simple questions requiring one-word answers. If I receive a simple answer from a student, most of my students now realise that I will come back with the question, 'Why do you say that...?' – requiring a much longer answer. Try to give out *some* easier questions, choosing those students who are less able to answer. It helps their self-esteem to know that they too can contribute. Also try to alternate as much as possible between girls and boys. Boys are naturally more likely to be forthcoming with answers, and if you are not careful, could dominate a class discussion. Another tip is to allow 'thinking time'. Do not accept the first hand that is raised; many students need time to think before they answer, and their response is just as valid as those who say the first thing that comes into their heads!

Writing out five key points from the last lesson

You need not take their responses in for marking, but they can be ticked off by the individual students as and when they are offered as answers. In this way all students participate. If the main activity is to be a practical activity, you may wish the students to write down their predictions of what they think will happen and why. In this case, they should name the sheets, keep them, and refer to them at the end, to verify if their predictions were correct or not.

True-false cards

These can be made easily out of green and red card. You can give the students a set of questions, with a true/false response. Again, by holding up the appropriate cards at the right moment, they all take part in the discussion, and by careful wording of questions you can have almost instant feedback of misconceptions.

In a typical one-hour lesson, the introduction should be no more than about 10 minutes.

Part 2 – the main activity

You next move on to the main activity. This may involve a demonstration, practical work, a video presentation, groupwork or any other activity that will constitute the bulk of the lesson. Aim to make this part of the lesson around 30 minutes, with an extra five minutes to give instructions.

Let us assume that the main activity is a practical session, as this will need the most classroom management. We will also assume that the students have a worksheet to accompany what they have to do, and that this worksheet contains extra work to do afterwards. You will need to give the class instructions in a clear fashion, the content of which will vary from practical experiment to practical experiment. However, your instructions should always contain the following:

(a)   Go over the procedure with the students so that everyone knows exactly what is expected. Ask individuals what they are to do, and praise them for their listening skills when they answer correctly.

(b)   Say what resources are available. You may need to tell them what to use (unless you are expecting them to choose the correct equipment if you are doing a practical activity). It is a good idea to spread out the resources around the room to avoid a jam in certain areas. Better still, appoint monitors to distribute Bunsen burners, gauzes, mats, eye protection and so on.

(c)   State your expectations regarding behaviour. The students will need to talk and possibly to move around to get to balances and so on. If this is the case, reiterate the safety rules.

(d)   Mention to the students any safety points regarding either the apparatus or the chemicals they are using, bearing in mind any risk assessments that are part of the scheme of work.

(e)   Make sure that the students know what they will be expected to have achieved by the end of the practical session.

(f)   Finally, give the students a time by when the task(s) should be completed (say, 30 minutes after you finish speaking) and stick to it! Ensure that they know what they should do regarding extension questions on the worksheet or another activity, if they finish early.

The main practical activity should last for the bulk of the lesson. During this time, you will need to be visiting each group to assist, encourage, answer questions, keep on task, and at the same time keep an eye on the other groups to ensure that they are carrying out the activity safely. Allow about three to five minutes for clearing away. It is a good idea to warn the students that they should be clearing away in, say, five minutes time. By placing time limits on the activities throughout the lesson, *you* control the pace of the lesson rather than the lesson (and the students!) controlling *you*.

    At the appropriate time for clearing away you may wish to use the monitors again, but make sure that you expect the students to clear up sensibly and quickly. All equipment should be returned to their trays, and counted in. Lost equipment is a serious matter, and might result in keeping students behind until it is found. Train your students to look after resources from the first time you see them. Things that tend to go astray are magnets, stopwatches, and anything that could be used in another class as a missile! Be vigilant.

Part 3 – the plenary session

At the end of the practical activity insist that the students should be back in their places, ready to go through the work, and to clarify what they have learned. Research has shown that the plenary session is frequently where the bulk of learning takes place, and so at least 15 minutes should be allocated for this activity. As with the introduction, there are several activities that can be used in the plenary session to consolidate what has been learned in the lesson. Some examples include:

▶ **Questions and answers**. This is a good way of starting, but, of course, you cannot ask everyone in the class and so you might find that many students slip through without any consolidation. Again, do not accept the first hand that is raised after a question; give the students thinking time. Extended discussions on their findings in the practical activity are useful because students have opportunities to air their views, articulate ideas and hear the ideas and views of others. If the concepts in the lesson focus are difficult to understand, the use of models and analogies to aid the students' understanding cannot be over emphasised.

▶ **Writing out five things they have learned today that they did not know before**. For some students this is quite a difficult exercise, especially if they have not paid enough attention at the start of the lesson. The list could be written in their notebooks, to be checked by you the next time that you mark their work. Another approach is to invite the students to share their list with the class. Most of the students will have learned the main points and written them down. Some students will have more advanced points that only a few students will have thought of. There may be one or two students, however, who have thought of relevant things they have learned in the lesson that no other student has learned. Depending upon their relevance and level, that student could be rewarded with a merit or housepoint for the most original fact learned.

▶ **A worksheet consolidating the learning objectives or lesson focus**. This can be a detailed set of questions or true/false questions either answered by the students individually or by the use of true-false cards. In a more able group you can use worksheets with appropriate questions to test what the students have learned. Another simple way of obtaining a response from the students is by using the 'traffic light' method. Three cards (red, yellow and green) are kept by the students in a pocket made by taping down the back page of their notebooks. One of these can be displayed on the table next to the student. If there is a green card, the student is happy with the lesson and feels confident about answering the consolidation sheet. If there is a yellow, the student may not be sure about one or two aspects of the work and may need your assistance. A red card, on the other hand, suggests that the student is having difficulties, and will need your assistance. By using cards in this way, you can move from student to student without having to deal with a sea of hands that can disrupt the most important part of the lesson. Furthermore, too many red or yellow cards will mean that the class as a whole will be having difficulty, and therefore it may be up to you to adjust your teaching accordingly.

Finally, you will need to go over the learning objectives again with the class before they leave, and tell them what they have learned. Compliment the class if they have worked well, or comment as they leave the room. Before dismissing the class, it is a good idea to preview the next lesson's topic so that they can look forward to the next thrilling instalment.

Dismissal should be in an orderly fashion. You may wish to dismiss students a table at a time, or dismiss those who have packed away and are ready and waiting, first. If you have timed the lesson correctly, the lesson should end at the correct time for dismissal, the class will go, you will need to ensure that the resources are cleared for the technician, and finally breathe a sigh of relief before the next class arrives.

A word about health and safety

In every scheme of work there should be a section on health and safety containing risk assessments for each experiment you do. You must adhere to the guidelines laid down by the scheme of work because you could find yourself found negligent if you disregard safety procedures and an accident occurs. Also check the laboratory rules of the department. These should be printed out and glued into every student's notebook. If you are trying something new, then it is important that you carry out a risk assessment on the experiment. Useful guidelines can be found in Cleapss literature and in 'Hazcards' – produced by Cleapss and used by many schools. Information on Hazcards can be downloaded from the Cleapss website (see Chapter 11), as can a large number of free publications. There is a charge for joining Cleapss, but your training school or your new school is more than likely to be a member.

A typical lesson plan using the three-part structure

This is a typical lesson plan that incorporates some of the ideas above. Perhaps you can see where there is differentiation and the use of literacy and numeracy (important for a class of less able students) and other factors discussed in this chapter. Some notes (in italics) have been included for you within key areas.

Example of a typical lesson with a year 7 class containing 20 students (16 boys and 4 girls), set 4 of 4. Three students have special needs statements. Most of the rest of the students are slow learners. The lesson lasts 50 minutes.

Lesson plan

Lesson context: Unit on Cells in the QCA Scheme of Work for year 7.

Lesson focus: Learning how to use a microscope.

Lesson objectives: 1. By the end of the lesson all students should be confident in handling a microscope safely, knowing the parts of the microscope and getting an image that is clear, bright and sharp.

2. By the end of the lesson, most students will know that the image is reversed.

3. By the end of the lesson some students will be able to work out the microscope's magnification. *[Three points, in increasing difficulty, showing differentiation.]*

Administration (5 minutes)

Introduction (10 mins)

1. Question and answer session on magnifying glasses, what is the students' understanding of magnification?

2. Demonstrate the correct use of a microscope to make observations under low magnification.

3. Go through worksheet, so they understand what they have to do.

   Resources: microscopes, lamps, acetate sheets with their names on, prepared slides.

Main activity (20 minutes)

1. Students are given microscopes and acetate sheets that have been prepared beforehand. The sheets are approximately the same size as a microscope slide so the students can concentrate on the microscope rather than on the making of

Using a microscope   Name:..............................

A   Draw a picture of an object you saw under the microscope. Add as much detail as you can.

B   Put the film with your name on it under the microscope so you can read it clearly. Now look at it through the microscope.
What do you have to do to your name to be able to read it?

....

....

Complete:
When I look down the microscope the image is........................... and

....

C Magnification
Magnification means how many times the microscope image is bigger than the real object. To work out the magnification you need to know the numbers on the eyepiece and the objective lens.

Number on the eyepiece is .... (line 10)

Number on the objective lens is..(line 4)

The magnification is the first number times the second number (like 10 x 4 - 40)

My magnification is: ....

Figure 4. Typical worksheet for the example lesson.

a slide. The acetate sheets were made simply by printing out the class list on sheets of acetate using Arial font at a size of 4 pt *[the students will be able to recognise their names easily at 4 pt, and will be able to recognise them also under the microscope, again taking away the need to recognise a biological sample. The reversal of the image is also more apparent]*.

2. Prepared slides are available for the majority of students. The worksheet that they use requires them to draw what they are seeing under the microscope. *[By their responses on the worksheet the teacher can see if objective 1 has been achieved]*.

3. Those students who have completed the drawings will carry on with sections B and C on the worksheet. In practice, almost every student will complete sections A and B, with a few completing section C.

Plenary (10 minutes)

1. A short discussion on the parts of the microscope and how to obtain an image

2. A brief question and answer session on sections B and C, so that the few students who did not get as far as section C will be able to complete their worksheet.

3. Distribute a second worksheet containing a diagram of a microscope with each part arrowed. The students are to put the right names for the parts at each arrow, using a list of the names with the letters jumbled. *[Unlike parts 1 and 2 of the plenary, here is an opportunity for all students to consolidate what they have learned. Literacy is an issue with less able students, and so exercises of this nature will help improve the use and spelling of scientific terms.]*

Dismissal and setting of homework (using the back of the worksheet, describe in their own words how they obtained a clear, bright, sharp image. This can be done either as a piece of extended prose or as a step-by-step set of instructions).

Summary

In this chapter we have addressed a typical science lesson in three parts – the introduction, the main activity and the plenary session and we have looked at an example of a lesson plan . You will have realised by now that there is a great deal of teacher preparation and input needed if a lesson is to be good. Of all the parts of the lesson, however, the most learning takes place in the plenary session. Get this right at the start, and, even with an average introduction and main activity, a great deal of learning will take place.

6

Organising your Paperwork and Time

One-minute summary – Nothing prepares the new teacher for the volume of paperwork that accompanies teaching in the classroom. Teachers need to organise time and paperwork in an effective way if they are not to be completely snowed under with a rising pile with less and less time to complete it. In this chapter you will learn a few simple tips that will at least reduce the problems arising from a paper overload.

Coping with the paper mountain

There is one golden rule to coping with paperwork. *Get organised*. You can usually cope with the paperwork if you make full use of eight simple filing systems, plus one extra file for your tutor group. These are:

▶ **Your mark book and planner** – together with your class registers these will contain all the day-to-day assessment marks and information to do with the students you teach, together with a diary for planning lessons, homework and other items.

▶ **A general file** – to house all the general items that you get on a daily basis – somewhere to place non-urgent items that you will need as reference material during the term or year. Timetables, pupil targets, duty rotas etc fall into this group.

▶ **Scheme of work** – including long term planning of lessons.

▶ **A Pending File** – somewhere to temporarily store urgent and semi-urgent material before dealing with it or filing it properly when you have time.

▶ **A to-do book** – to make daily lists.

▶ **Your diary**.

▶ **Boxes** – one for each class set of books.

▶ **Filing cabinet** – for worksheets, tutor group files, and long-term storage.

▶ **Pastoral file** for your tutor group.

Mark book and planner

In the modern computer age, the mark book still has a major place. Although test results entered on a computer allow worthwhile statistical analysis of data, for day-to-day recording the mark book still reigns supreme. It provides an instant record of attendance, homework records, lesson plans, test results and so on. It does not need a power supply, and never crashes losing data. On the market at the moment are some excellent teacher planners, and it is well worth investing in one of these. An example of a useful style is given in Figure 5 below:

Day.................................... Date:		
Pd Class	Lesson Planned	Homework
1		
2		
3		
4		
5		

Figure 5. A useful layout for a planner.

Planners have a day-to-a-page spread with space for each lesson focus – homework, and after school activities (e.g. meetings). The rear of the planner is usually devoted to a mark book or class register. In addition it will include a year planner as well. Usually, however, a double page A4 spread will be insufficient to include all the marks, including attendance marks, for the whole class for a year. To alleviate this problem, write in your class list every other page, and in the pages between, cut the page at the left hand side to remove the column for names. Then when you turn over the page you can use the same class list for more than one page. Many schools now expect that each class you take is registered before the lesson (an effective tactic to reduce truancy). You can use the one double-page spread for the register, and the other for recording marks or grades.

Year 7 set 1	Sc SATs Yr 6	CATs scores	Reading test	Pref. Learning style	Target min level	Hwk 8 Sept	Hwk 15 Sept	Hwk 22 Sept	Hwk 29 Sept	Test 1 (%)	Hwk 7 Oct
AMPERE Anna	5	121	120	Mu	7	A	A	B	A	72	E
BUNSEN, Bertie	5	124	122	Bk	7	B	A	B	C	68	A
CALORIE, Charles	4	98	100	lp	6	A	B	B	C	69	B
DUODENUM, David	5	108	108	la	7	C	B	B	C	71	C
ERBIUM, Enid	5	124	126	Bk	7	B	B	C	D	54	E
FARADAY, Frances	5	120	122	Ma	7	B	B	B	C	78	C
GLASSWARE, Gertie	5	114	118	Bk	7	C	B	B	C	62	B
HYDROCARBON, Henry	5	111	105	Ma	7	B	A	C	B	61	E
ILEUM, Iris	4	100	99	lp	6	B	C	B	B	71	A
JUPITER, Janice	5	117	122	lp	7	Abs	C	B	B	65	B
KRYPTON, Katie	5	128	129	Ma	7	B	B	B	C	84	E
LIMESTONE, Linda	5	106	110	Ma	6	B	B	A	B	63	
MOLYBDENUM, Max	5	100									

Figure 6. A section of a typical mark book.

The planner is an invaluable aid to planning work for a week or two ahead. I usually sit down with the technician on a weekly basis, with my planner, and discuss the forthcoming week's lessons. If there are problems over equipment, for example, clashes with other classes, then these can, as a result of forward planning, be flagged up early so that alternatives can be found. Also, if equipment needs to be ordered (e.g. a heart or lungs for dissection) then you can use the planner to identify needs weeks ahead. Moreover, a well used planner will then double as a record book of lessons and topics covered, so that reference can be made to old planners if records of homework set, or topics covered, need to be referred to.

A general file
This should be a ring binder divided into sections. A good start is to have the first section devoted to all the general information that needs to be kept close to hand – including pupil targets and data, minutes of meetings waiting to be filed, individual education plans for students with special needs and so on. Divide the

second section into months, either with dividers or polythene pockets. Starting with September through to July, these can contain items that come into school that need dealing with at certain times of the year. For example, information about a training day in February that arrives in October can be put into the February pocket. It will be to hand when you need it after glancing at your diary at the end of January and discovering that you will need the information about the training day that you had long forgotten was going to happen!

Scheme of work

This will, more than likely, be the departmental document issued to you by your departmental head. However, as a working document you should be encouraged to add your notes to each lesson or set of lessons (in pencil if need be) so that you can keep track of lessons that went well, or things to avoid in future. Don't forget that you will probably be using the same, or at least similar scheme for several years and so any notes made this year will help in subsequent years.

A pending file

This is a box file or tray that holds items that need to be dealt with either urgently or at least semi-urgently. In this file should be items that either need to be acted on or filed away permanently. Try to clear your pending file at least weekly. In-out trays are useful only if you have an area where there is a desk not likely to be disturbed. An 'In' tray doubles as your 'Pending file'.

To-do list

This is vital. A reporter's notebook or small exercise book should always be close to hand, with enough pages for at least a page a day for the term. The 'To-do' lists will include all the minor items that crop up throughout the day.

▶ *Never* write phone numbers on scraps of paper that will get lost.

▶ *Never* remove pages from your To-do book. You do not know when you will need that address you were given last week.

▶ *Always* use your To-do book to record anything that you will need to remember to do throughout the day.

▶ *Always* try to clear your To-do book daily, before you go home from school.

▶ *Always*, weekly, transfer any important data (telephone numbers, addresses, contacts etc) to your diary.

Diary

Planners or mark books are of great use, but tend to be large and bulky. A diary is also useful to keep, containing important information regarding dates such as parents' evenings meetings and so on. It is useful to duplicate some information by copying it into your planner, for example, information that has a bearing on your lessons taught such as dates of school trips when students may miss lessons. In this way appropriate information will always be at hand.

Book boxes

As a science teacher, you will probably be teaching science to around eight or ten different classes throughout the week. Keeping track of books is difficult, especially if, like in many schools, your department has a particular colour for its books. Often students will place books in the wrong piles and claim that they are 'lost'. This means that valuable lesson time is used up in trying to track books that are not in the place they should be. If all your books are the same size or colour, then there are several ways in which you can identify them immediately:

▶ Coloured spines. Invest in several colours of sticky tape (such as insulating tape) and tape the spines of books in each class with the same colour. In this way, rogue books in the wrong pile can be identified immediately.

▶ Large letters on the cover – e.g. 10 set 2 – written in the top left hand corner in thick marker pen opposite the student's name.

▶ A coloured sticker on the book – one colour per class taught.

A book box. Invest in boxes or trays that are clearly marked with the name of each class, and if possible, colour-coded. Train the students always to return their books to the appropriate box.

Filing cabinet

Filing cabinets should contain items that need long-term storage. If you have a three-drawer cabinet, then the top drawer can be used for materials that need more frequent access such as worksheets used in class or in your tutor group. The top drawer should be used because it will avoid unnecessary bending down or crouching to retrieve items. Lower drawers should contain long-term storage such as student records, minutes of meetings and anything filed from your pending file. Try to keep your files in alphabetical order so that retrieval time is cut to a minimum. Filing cabinets should be cleared out once a year (usually in July), to remove unwanted material and to create space.

Pastoral file

This is dealt with in Chapter 9.

Handling post

Depending upon your role in the school you will either get a great deal of post, or be inundated! Much of your post will consist of unsolicited circulars offering software, books, worksheets, courses and so on. There is one golden rule when handling post: *it should pass through your hands once and once only*. After this initial sorting it is either filed (in your pending file if you do not have time to file it properly) or else binned. If unsolicited post is kept 'in case' then you will end up with huge piles of paper in which important documents will invariably get lost or mixed up with the junk mail you have accumulated.

Time management

During your induction year you should be on a reduced timetable. This will give you some respite as far as workload is concerned. However, you will still find that time has to be planned carefully if you are to avoid getting snowed under with work. In this section we will concentrate on marking and other forms of assessment.

Assessment and planning

Marking

By far the most time-consuming task is in marking work, followed closely by planning lessons. It is essential that you get into a routine when marking – try to ensure that when you set work there is sufficient time for you to mark the assignments between lessons. There must be an appropriate balance between having a reasonable turn-round time for your own sanity, and in getting feedback swiftly to the students.

Setting homework is best done 'backwards'; firstly, check your timetable to see when the best times are for you to *mark* the work. It may be that you have some non-contact periods on a Tuesday straight after having a year 7 class so it would make sense for them to hand in their work then, so that it can be marked immediately afterwards.

Secondly, assuming that year 7 will be handing their work in during this lesson, which lesson will you set it? It may be the day before, a Monday, or possibly even the week before. Either way, you are *collecting it* in when you have *the time to mark it* and to get feedback to the students quickly. Treat your other classes in the same way. Set homework appropriately so you can avoid having to mark work in the evenings or after school when you know you will be busy. Avoid time after school when you have meetings, or evenings when you have other engagements. Try to avoid, on principle, Friday after school, and on Sundays. You need at least one day of complete rest and recuperation before starting back on Monday!

The type of marking you do can also affect the time you spend on it. Your school, or at least your department, will have a marking policy, and you should adhere to it. Marking work means more than just correction. Indeed, correcting every spelling mistake so that each page is a mass of red ink is not only time-consuming but demotivating, especially to a less able student. It is more important to give a formative comment (i.e. a comment suggesting ways in which the student can improve) and/or a grade for effort plus a level, if appropriate. Try to mark thoroughly in this way at least once a fortnight. Intermittent marking can be less thorough as long as the students are happy that you give them feedback regarding their progress. This could even be verbal if necessary.

Preparation

So you have arrived at a routine of marking work weekly at specified times. Next you have to think about preparation. You will find that it will be impossible to prepare lessons as thoroughly as you would have done as a student on placement. Time is just not available to do so. As far as long-term planning is concerned, this should be dealt with by the departmental scheme of work. Therefore, make use of the scheme of work in your medium-term (i.e. weekly) planning to ensure that the lesson objectives are covered appropriately, plan your activities and let the laboratory technicians know what equipment you require. If you are able to sit down with the technician for half an hour during a non-contact period, or after school, then this is even better as an experienced technician will be able to advise you on what is available, and of course, what works well!

It should take you at least the same amount of time to prepare lessons each week as to mark the students' work. You need to bear this in mind when planning your weekly time allocation for this activity. However, if you are teaching several groups in a year cohort, you will find that preparation will be reduced, as often the same lesson will be taught to more than one class, with some adjustment for differentiation and so on. Also, after your first year, you can look back on your notes in your old planner (*never* throw them away) and plan that much more quickly.

Assessments

Other time-consuming activities include setting tests. In many departments the scheme of work includes module tests or unit assessments. However, if you have to set your own, try to cut down the time needed to set, administer and mark the test. There are various ways in which this can be done.

▶ Make sure that the total marks allocated for the test is a round number like 20, 50 or so on. This will mean that calculating a percentage mark is much easier.

▶ Try to include a level for each question. Then the tests can be used for evidence when ascertaining a level in the National Curriculum so that 'levelling' becomes easier. Levels may be obtained by cross-referencing with the scheme of work or by using SATs-type questions that have already been levelled. Students' levels, and even 'sub-levels' can be determined by this method.

▶ Write the test to take around half the lesson and, instead of collecting it in to mark, ask the students to swap papers and mark their neighbours'. This has the advantage that answers can be discussed in the group and the students have instant feedback. The disadvantage, however, is that you cannot guarantee that the student has not 'doctored' his or her own mark or that of his or her friend.

▶ Multiple-choice tests where the student chooses the correct answer from a group of four or five alternatives need more time to set up, and to produce five plausible alternatives is time consuming. Also, they suffer a disadvantage in that they do not allow free-response answers. However, marking is exceptionally easy as the answers can be completed on a grid, and by means of an acetate template placed over the answer sheets with the incorrect answers blocked out, the number of correct responses can be counted quickly. Furthermore, for large numbers of students the answers can be plotted onto sheets designed for optical readers so that they can be imported into computer software for immediate analysis.

▶ Always file tests and any question banks you have used. Syllabuses *do* change, but the vast majority of tests and questions can be used several times without a great deal of change. If the tests are stored on disc this is even better, as new tests can be generated by cutting and pasting of questions.

Don't forget, any time spent now writing tests or assessments should not be seen as a one-off exercise – it should be seen as an investment in saving time in the future.

Summary

When it comes to organising paperwork, aim to adhere to three simple rules:

1. 'A place for everything, and everything in its place.'
2. Keep documents that are in regular use accessible.
3. File away any documents that you need to keep but are used or needed only infrequently. Bin everything else.

7

Good Demonstrations

One-minute summary – Modern science teaching emphasises the investigative approach to the subject through hands-on practical work – and rightly so. Students often learn better by 'doing'. However, there are times when, for safety reasons, or possibly through a lack of equipment or resources, the teacher demonstrates to the students a particular experiment or series of experiments. In this chapter we will be looking at what makes a good demonstration and you will be given an example of a typical demonstration to illustrate some of the principles discussed.

A good demonstration

It is unfortunate that the art of demonstrating experiments has waned a great deal in recent years, yet the good demonstration plays an important role in the effective science teacher's repertoire of skills. In this chapter we will firstly look at what makes a good demonstration, with due emphasis on safety. For some topics good demonstrations are as good, and sometimes better, than experiments performed by the students themselves. Bad demonstrations are worse than useless – the students switch off, get bored and end up with the assumption that 'Mr Bloggs' experiments never work...'. Secondly, I will talk you through a couple of demonstrations that are very common and, whatever your discipline, you will probably find yourself having to do these at some stage in your first year of teaching. Use them as examples and eventually develop your own style of presentation.

Before you start

▶ Look at the topic you will be covering and decide which areas are best suited to students themselves carrying out practical work and which are suited more to demonstration. It may be that all the activities in a particular topic are suited to the students' own investigative work. However, there may be some topics, such as radioactivity, where demonstrations are performed almost exclusively because of obvious safety considerations.

▶ Next, decide just what concepts you are trying to get across to your audience. Then *stick to them*. Many a good demonstration has gone wrong or worse still becomes a hazard because the teacher tries something out for the first time in front of the class just because the student in the front row is egging him or her on.

▶ Look up any safety aspects of the demonstration in CLEAPSS literature or Hazcards. Don't forget that a demonstration is more likely to be hazardous because of the very fact that you are performing the experiment as a demonstration. Make proper use of safety equipment – safety screen and spectacles/safety goggles for the students and yourself.

▶ Finally, practise at least twice on your own, either during a non-contact period when the laboratory is free, or after school. A good idea is to have someone experienced with you to support you – a head of department or a laboratory technician. Practise the experiment until you know, not only how to perform the demonstration, but also the outcome, including the questions to the students, ensuring that your objectives are covered.

During the demonstration

▶ Position the class around the demonstration bench so that they have a good view, but are not so close as to be within a 'danger zone'. Make sure that they are comfortable, sitting on laboratory stools for instance, in proper rows, so that they are less likely to fidget. They may need their laboratory notebooks in order to take notes on results as you perform the experiment.

▶ Make sure that your demonstration table/bench is free from clutter. The technician will have brought the equipment in but it is up to you to position the apparatus/chemicals as you wish.

▶ During the actual experiment ask questions of the class in order to direct their thinking towards your objectives for that lesson. A good idea to keep their interest is to drop the occasional anecdote or even joke into your patter.

▶ If you need to use the blackboard during the demonstration, try to have completed as much of the written work as possible prior to the demonstration. Writing down results can easily be done by a chosen student. The reason for this is that you should try to face your class as much as possible – one miscreant fiddling with potentially harmful equipment or chemicals behind your back could be potentially dangerous.

▶ Depending on the safety considerations of the experiment you are demonstrating, it is good practice to invite one or two students to help you. Make sure, however, that each lesson you choose someone different so that everyone has a chance of helping.

▶ Don't forget that above all a good demonstration is meant to be enjoyable – not just for your class but also for you. Enjoy what you do. Demonstrating is the nearest thing in teaching to a 'song and dance' act – you are an *actor* performing to your *audience*. Make sure that those in the stalls get their money's worth!

After the demonstration

▶ As with the normal lesson cycle, recap what the students have seen and relate the observations to the objectives at the start of the lesson. In a three-part lesson, where the demonstration makes up the main activity, the third part will be a normal plenary session.

▶ Make sure that the students return to their places in an orderly fashion.

▶ Try to engineer a plenary activity that the students can engage in with little input from you, at least at the start. (For example, to copy the results from their rough notebooks into their exercise books, to write an account of the experiment, etc.) You then have a breathing space after issuing your instructions in which you can tidy up your table and make everything safe for removal by the technician.

An example of a demonstration

Here is a demonstration chosen to illustrate some of the above points.

The reactions of the alkali metals with water

Equipment needed –   large trough (at least 30 cm diameter – preferably 40 cm) of water
one bottle of universal Indicator
Bunsen burner and splint
test tube
tile
tongs
knife
alkali metals
safety screen and safety spectacles for the class

The alkali metals usually come in small jars of oil containing lumps of the metal that have to be cut into smaller pieces before they can be used in this demonstration.

Safety

▶ Use the safety screen throughout. There is seldom any problem with lithium but both sodium and particularly potassium have been known to explode in contact with water. It is important to add that the experiment demonstrating the reaction between potassium and water has been withdrawn by some Local Education Authorities. Check with your science team leader before attempting it.

▶ Make sure that the trough of water is placed to one side. Cut pieces of the metals in front of the class so that they can see the metals tarnishing in air – and their softness. The use of a flexicam here will enable a video image of the small pieces to be transmitted onto a large screen so that the students can see the tarnishing much better. Use the tongs and knife to cut. The pieces should be no larger than a grain of rice.

▶ Old alkali metal pieces have a great deal of tarnishing on them. On sodium, for example, most of the white coating is sodium carbonate. If a piece of sodium with any coating (tarnish or oil) adhering to it is added to water it is more likely to explode because of the hot spot created by the coating. Therefore, make sure that the pieces you use have any tarnish or oil removed.

▶ Replace any unused metal into the jars before adding the pieces to the water. Place the jars out of the way.

▶ When adding the pieces – stand clear after adding each piece. Do not add more than two or three pieces of each metal.

▶ Between demonstrating each metal make sure that you change the water in the trough. You wish to investigate the reaction between the metal and water, not the metal and a solution of a less reactive metal hydroxide – which is much more violent!

▶ At the end of the three metals demonstration it is good practice to drop the knife, tongs and tile in the water to ensure that any pieces of alkali metal on them are not left lying around.

▶ Any superfluous alkali metal pieces can be disposed of by adding them to ethanol where they will dissolve slowly and safely.

During the demonstration

Provide your class with a grid showing the name of the metal, its relative softness, how it is stored, its reaction with water, the gas evolved and the properties of the liquid left. The students can fill this in as you go through the demonstration. If you are studying periodicity you can also include the next two metals, rubidium and caesium, in the table, and ask the students to predict their properties as you clear away.

Take each metal in turn and perform the demonstration with due regard to safety. Students are usually in awe of a metal that reacts with water in such a way. Start with lithium so that you leave the best till last! Each time, at the end of the reaction, test the solution with indicator (a volunteer can do this) and note the violet colour of a strong alkali.

Testing the hydrogen positively is difficult. With lithium it is safer as you can trap a small piece of the metal in an upside down test tube and then test the gas in the test tube with a lighted splint to hear the 'pop'. With sodium, it is more difficult. One way I have found successful is to get the class absolutely silent, and after waiting until the sodium globule has nearly disappeared, light it and hear the faint 'pop'. Do not attempt this with a larger piece of sodium – it will more than likely explode. As for the potassium – you will hear the hydrogen's 'pop' as it spontaneously ignites.

For an anecdote to accompany this demonstration, I use one that happened to me when I was at school. We had a very nervous student teacher perform this demonstration for us. The laboratory was very old-fashioned with a large earthenware sink at each end of the demonstration bench. After completing the reaction with potassium he stretched over to reach the indicator bottle, and inadvertently knocked the jar of potassium into the sink where it smashed releasing two or three lumps of the metal into the water puddles at the bottom of the sink. Panicking, to put out the flames, he turned on the tap... If you leave the anecdote at this point – you will be able to tell those students who have paid attention – they will be the first to cringe. The explosion caused the destruction of the sink and part of the bench. Amazingly no one was hurt.

Incidentally, the BBC Bitesize GCSE Revision video shows a sequence including both the reactions of rubidium and caesium on water.

Summary

Doing a good demonstration needs practice much in the same way as a stage performance. In this chapter we have looked at what makes a good demonstration. Do not forget that demonstrations have their place in the curriculum but cannot take the place of investigative work carried out by the students themselves. Students learn best by doing, but if investigative work is not possible, a good demonstration is the next best thing.

8

Professional Development

One-minute summary – As a new member of a profession you are entitled to professional development throughout your career. Many schools today have been given the Investors in People Award, and it is their duty to support and protect you throughout your time in the school. This award is a good indication of the support you will receive, and may be something to consider when applying for posts. In this chapter we will be mainly dwelling on the sort of support that you will receive as you enter the profession, with some indication of the sort of professional development that you can expect to receive afterwards.

The career entry profile

This is completed during your teacher training, and it is this document that is taken to your first teaching post. The profile is split into three main sections:

Section A – A summary of your teacher training
This is simply a proforma indicating your personal details, what training you did, where, and for how long.

Section B – Your strengths and areas for development in your induction period
During your Initial Teacher Training (ITT) there will be some areas in which you will excel. Here you will include any areas in which you feel that you have strengths that may be of use in your new school. As an example, one of my previous students had an expertise in ICT, and used his skills a great deal in using computing with his classes. He used datalogging, spreadsheets and Internet research with many of his groups and fulfilled many of the ICT curriculum statements in the programme of study almost single-handedly. He was able to offer these skills to his new school, as they wanted help in developing the school web site. The proforma does not include the term 'weakness' but 'area for development'. This implies that if you are weak in a particular aspect, for example, you are a biology specialist with a lack of subject knowledge in physics, then this weakness is not seen as permanent, but that with support and training, this area can and will be developed during your induction year.

This section has to be agreed between you and your ITT tutor. If you are unhappy about any section, then what is written down is negotiable.

Section C – Revised objectives and action plans for your induction year
In this section you will be outlining how you will undertake to address your areas for development in your new school. As a newly qualified teacher you will be

designated a tutor in your new school, and it will be his or her responsibility to complete this section with you. You will identify the training you will need, the cost to the school and the success criteria of the training. You will also set targets by which any developments should be completed. Again, this is a negotiable document which you and your tutor will sign, only when both of you are happy with its contents. This section of the profile is important because not only does it set out your intentions over the induction year with regard to your development, but it also safeguards you as it also sets out the school's responsibility in meeting your training needs.

Your induction year

The induction period is designed to ensure that all newly qualified teachers are supported and appropriately trained during their first year of teaching. In this way, further professional development builds on a firm foundation. The induction period lasts three terms, and it must be completed if you are to continue teaching in a maintained school in England. You need to be proactive in planning your induction programme in order that it meets your particular needs. In any induction programme there will be two main strands. Firstly, you will receive an individual programme of professional development and monitoring; secondly, you will be assessed against national induction standards to ensure quality teachers are entering the profession.

In your induction year you can expect the following:

▶ **A 90% timetable**. In your school you should be given only 90% of the teaching load of a teacher with no extra responsibilities, above the normal non-contact periods the school allocates. This extra time should not be taken for other activities such as covering for absent colleagues, but should be used for your own development, as outlined in your career entry profile.

▶ **Funding.** Your school will receive substantial funding to help you through the induction period. This will include the costs incurred when releasing you from teaching for in-service training.

▶ **An induction tutor.** Your tutor will have the most influence over your induction period and he or she will have day-to-day responsibility to ensure that your induction period is going to plan.

▶ **An individualised programme.** Your career entry profile needs to be presented to the head teacher and your tutor on entering your new school. Your training will reflect your strengths and needs covered in your profile. You will meet with your tutor to discuss how you will meet your targets, and what kind of training you need to receive.

▶ **Teaching observation.** As a newly qualified teacher, expect to be observed at least twice a term by your tutor, and at other times by your head of department. The review period afterwards is meant to be non-threatening and is designed to enable you to improve. Do not forget that everyone has lessons that occasionally go badly. The more observations you receive, the more likely it is that the percentage of good or better lessons will be higher.

▶ **A programme of professional development.** Your tutor and you will draw up a programme to include areas of the school in which you have an interest. Activities will include job-shadowing of more experienced colleagues, observation of lessons taken by experienced staff, training outside the school, visiting other schools and establishments, and meetings with your tutor and head of department.

▶ **Termly assessment.** You and your tutor or head of department will meet with the head teacher once a term to review your progress, focusing especially on your progress towards meeting the National Induction Standards. A report of the first two meetings will be sent to the LEA (or for independent schools to the Independent Schools Council Teacher Induction Panel (ISCTIP), to inform them of your progress.

▶ **Additional support in case of difficulty.** If, at any point, your tutor or head of department feels that you may be in danger of not meeting the induction standard by the end of your induction period, the LEA or ISCTIP will be informed and additional support will be given to you. If there is insufficient progress at one stage of your induction year do not feel that inevitably you will fail! You will find that everyone will work positively to ensure that you meet the standards required of you.

▶ **A named contact at the LEA/ISCTIP.** If you have concerns regarding your induction year, your first port of call is, of course, your tutor or head teacher. However, if you still feel that your concern has not been dealt with satisfactorily, you will be given a contact name of someone at either the LEA or ISCTIP at the start of your induction period who can advise you.

▶ **A recommendation on completing your induction period.** After term three, your head teacher will inform the LEA/ISCTIP whether or not, in his/her opinion, you have fulfilled the national standards. The LEA/ISCTIP will then decide and write to you formally of the decision. They will also inform your head teacher, and the General Teaching Council.

Do not forget, however, that it is your induction year. Be proactive in ensuring that your needs are met. Your school is being funded to provide your induction year for you. The funds received should go directly to your training needs to ensure that the induction standards are met, and that your year is successful. The high standards of professionalism that are expected of you means that you need to show some responsibility for making the programme succeed. In particular, you are expected to play an active role in all aspects of your programme.

▶ Make yourself familiar with the induction standards, so that you know what is expected of you by the end of your programme.

▶ Review Section B of your career entry profile and be ready to discuss your training needs in order to meet the induction standards.

▶ Discuss your career entry profile with your head teacher and tutor.

▶ Plan your own programme of support and assessment with your tutor and participate fully in the programme, gathering evidence to help you towards your assessments.

▶ Review your progress towards the Induction Standards. Raise any concerns earlier rather than later.

Further professional development

Development and training does not stop at the end of the induction year. Throughout your career you will be offered training in all aspects of the teaching profession. All maintained schools in England and Wales have designated five days annually as compulsory in-service-training days, the subjects on each day being decided by the school. In addition to this, each school has a training budget that is allocated to individuals for their own professional development. Each department has a development plan for the next year indicating training needs. In good schools individuals will also have a plan for the coming year where individual training needs are highlighted. You may, for example, wish to be trained in tutoring children and pastoral care, with the intention of pursuing promotion to year head or house leader in the future. Training like this should be made available to you.

Performance management

A good school will have a system in place by which staff are regularly monitored and supported. A good system will have the following aspects:

▶ Regular meetings with your line manager to discuss progress and standards.
▶ An individual development plan.

▶ Monitoring of exercise books, marking and teacher observation by your line manager.

▶ A yearly review of your progress and standards by your line manager.

As a head of department I was responsible for the professional development of the teachers in my team. In turn, I was reviewed by my line manager, the head teacher, although in some areas it would be one of the deputy head teachers instead who would be the manager. In my present role, my line manager is the head teacher and governors.

Such a system is vital if you are to accumulate enough evidence to eventually, given enough experience, progress through the Upper-Pay-Spine Threshold. For many years, the only way in which teachers could progress through the profession and be remunerated accordingly, was to take on more and more of an administrative role and do less teaching. Thus, many excellent teachers were promoted out of the classroom. The government decided to develop an upper-pay-spine to keep excellent teachers in the classroom. In order to pass through the threshold, you have to have at least eight years' experience, complete a detailed proforma and collect evidence of meeting a high standard of professionalism. Your head teacher will interview you and decide whether or not you meet the criteria. Although you will not be in this position for some time yet, it is prudent to keep a file of evidence supporting you in your professionalism as a teacher, so that completion of the standards is much easier. Things like examination results of classes you have taught, value-added results at both Key Stages 3 and 4 and post-16, contributions to school life, pastoral care etc, all make up a bank of evidence. Even thank-you letters from parents will help. I have a 'positive file' now, in which I keep evidence like this. It also helps to read through it sometimes, when you are feeling stressed and down, to realise that you are not so bad at your job after all!

Summary

The transition from Initial Teacher Training to the induction period signifies just a start to a new phase of your career as a teacher. The completion of your induction marks yet another step in your progress as a professional educator. You must appreciate that your professional development will carry on for the whole of your career. However, the emphasis is on *your* professional development. Be responsible for planning it and ensuring that it meets your needs, not only simply to meet standards laid down by government, but also to be the best teacher you possibly can be.

9

Pastoral Care and Parents

One-minute summary – As well as the academic duties of a teacher there is a great emphasis placed on pastoral care in the classroom. In this section you will be finding out a little about the role of the group tutor, and in meeting with and reporting to parents.

Your tutor group

It is quite usual that a newly qualified teacher will be allocated a tutor group in his or her induction year. Part of your professional development will include some pastoral work, and in many ways, this work can be most rewarding. Your school is likely to be organised pastorally in one of two ways, either as houses, or as year groups. Houses are arranged vertically throughout the school, so that each house has a house leader who, along with his or her tutors, is responsible pastorally for all the students in that house from the year 7 students fresh from their primary schools through to the sixth-formers. In the year group system, the Year Leader will have a team of tutors in a particular year group e.g. year 7, who are responsible for that particular year cohort as they progress through the school. In most schools the tutor remains with his or her group throughout their time in school. In this way, he or she becomes expert in all aspects of pastoral care throughout the school (for example, induction in year 7, careers information in year 9, exam preparation in years 11, 12 and 13 and so on). Also, by the end of five or seven years, you will know the students really well, and of course, they will get to know you.

I still keep in touch with many of my students who are now married with families of their own (some of whose children I teach!). This is one of the most rewarding parts of being a tutor – getting to know the students as people, rather than as examination statistics.

What does a tutor do? It is difficult to tell – but suffice it to say you are the first person to whom either your tutees or parents should come when they wish to contact the school. Among the duties that the tutor undertakes will include:

Administration tasks

Marking a daily attendance register is a legal document and a requirement of every school. You must make sure that the register is accurate and clear, whether paper based or done by optical card readers, is accurate and clear. In the event of a prosecution of a parent for non-attendance, the school register may be used as evidence, so any inaccuracies will not be acceptable. In addition to the register, you will be required to distribute notices, letters, and collect returns from the parents. You may be required to collect money for trips or other events. Absences of students need to be covered by a note from the parents. Notes should be retained in a pastoral file. This is a simple lever arch file containing polypockets for each of your students. Notes and letters from parents, and records of telephone messages can be popped into the file easily in each child's polypocket, for easy retrieval if required.

Pastoral work

▶ **Tutor interviews**. As a tutor, you will be responsible for the children in your care. In many schools tutors have a non-contact period to meet with their students either individually or in small groups each term to discuss targets and progress.

▶ **Tutor periods**. You will be allocated at least one period per week as a tutor period. In this period you will teach your group as a tutor group rather than a normal teaching set. The content of the work will be set by your year head or head of house and the tutor team. Many schools use tutor time as a vehicle to deliver the statutory citizenship curriculum that has now become compulsory in maintained schools. Usually there are a large number of resources provided by your year head or head of house, so preparation of lessons is kept to a minimum.

▶ **Dealing with referrals**. As tutor, you will receive referrals from the staff who teach your group if there are problems over behaviour that have gone beyond what the normal classroom teacher wishes to deal with, or, for your information, if one of your students has been referred to a senior member of staff. You will need to keep a record of problems in your pastoral file so that a formal referral can be made to your pastoral leader in your team meeting.

▶ **Other tutor activities**. These will include supporting your group in sporting and other events and will also include accompanying them on trips. You may also wish to contribute to tutor group, house group or year group assemblies.

Reports

As a tutor you will be required to write reports for the students in your group as well as the students to whom you teach science. In a science report your comments will concentrate mostly on academic progress, the quality of class work, homework and practical work, and set targets that the student should meet in the future. Your tutor comment should reflect the general progress of the student based on your tutor interviews and on reports and referrals from teaching staff. Absence records and contribution to tutor activities may also be included. It is important to include as much detail as you can; reports are of great use not only to parents, but also copies kept are invaluable to the school as it provides formal evidence and proof of a student's progress. Your induction tutor, head of department or pastoral head will help you with report writing.

Parents' evenings

These take place either termly or annually for each year group you teach. Parents make an appointment with you using a proforma. Appointments last usually for about five minutes, and so the way in which you present information to them needs to be tight. After an initial greeting, you will need to comment on behaviour, standard of work and progress. Be honest – if George is underachieving it is likely that his parents will have heard the same report from his other teachers. If you know the parents' names, (they may be different from their child if there has been a remarriage), then this indicates that you have been professional enough to take the trouble to find this out. Try to stick to time; leave a couple of minutes at the end of the interview for the parents to comment, or to suggest a way in which George can improve. Finally, thank them for coming, and as they leave, stand and offer a handshake. Do not forget manners – you are a professional after all.

You will find that the vast majority of parents are charming, and show a great deal of gratitude for what you are doing for their offspring. However, very occasionally you may encounter a difficult parent. Never put yourself in a position where a parent may show less that the greatest of respect for you. If there is ever any problem, terminate the interview immediately and refer the matter to your head of department, or the head teacher.

Summary

Being a good teacher takes hard work; being a good tutor takes hard work *and* dedication. In this chapter we have had a brief look at the role of a group tutor. Do not forget: your relationship with your tutor group is one of the most important in a school. You will be with them at least twice a day plus other times. If you maintain a good relationship throughout their school career, many will cease to be simply your students – they will become friends.

10

Using Computers

One-minute summary – During your initial teacher training, in tour induction year and throughout your career, the computer will be a vital tool to aid teaching and learning. In this chapter you will be learning how the computer is used in the science department and how it can enhance not only your teaching, but also the students' learning.

What can I expect?

In schools today, the computer/student ratio has never been better. The vast majority of students you will encounter will be computer-literate and many will be more knowledgeable than you. Schools generally have computer rooms furnished with 20–30 machines, enough for individual work, or at least one computer between two students. Larger schools have several rooms of this type, which can be booked if you wish to take a class in there.

Many schools are now moving from desktop machines over to laptops (for convenience and portability) and even palmtops for simple word processing, although security poses a problem with the latter as they are easily pocketed. The main software used is almost invariably Microsoft Office Suite – now probably the standard in the business world. In larger schools they may have some AppleMac machines as an alternative. You may still find, however, tucked away in a corner some old BBC machines or an Acorn RISC PC or two. Schools moved away from Acorn quite a few years ago – a pity because they had a better operating system – but found themselves stuck with large amounts of software that PCs could not run. As an interim measure they used the RISC system that could operate both.

In most schools now the computers are networked to a large server so that students are able to have their own bit of space for storage, meaning that the use of floppy discs (potentially a virus problem) is kept to a minimum. Many students also enjoy the allocation of a free email address. It is becoming increasingly popular now to email work to teachers and to use videoconferencing facilities and instant messaging services.

If you are applying for a post in a school and wish to know a little about its use of ICT, a good starting point is the school's website. A well-constructed site is indicative of a well run ICT department. Either the department wrote the site itself, suggesting a great deal of expertise, or, if contracted out to a webmaster, shows that they take the image of the school and its use of ICT seriously enough to pay for the service.

How are computers used in science classes?

Computers may be used for all sorts of applications, but the rule is simple: does the use of the computer enhance teaching and learning? If so, go ahead. If, on the other hand, you are using the computer simply as a gimmick, then there is probably a more effective way of teaching that particular point. In normal science classes, the use of computers can be split into six areas:

1. Simulation

There are many scientific phenomena that are either too dangerous or too difficult (requiring specialist equipment) to attempt in the laboratory. Computers may be able to use simulation to help here. A networked program shared in a computer room may be able to show what happens to the yield of ammonia manufactured in the Haber process, for example, if the pressure and temperature of the reaction are changed. Students will get an instant response from the machine, and so their understanding of chemical equilibria will be enhanced. Software is available for a huge number of simulations. You will no doubt receive unsolicited circulars about what is available, some at a price, however, and it will be up to you which you might like to try. Some software is available as a trial version – with the full version being available after paying a site licence.

2. Revision software

This is normally used by students preparing for GCSE or post-16 examinations. However, revision software can be purchased for use at all levels especially at the end of Key Stage 3, where SATs-type questions are available. Revision can be a boring exercise, and anything that keeps the students on task is of benefit. If your students like using computers, this is an excellent way to revise.

3. The Internet

The Internet is mostly useful as a research tool. It is of particular use in obtaining the higher levels in GCSE and A-level coursework, as higher marks are only awarded if students are able to have used some background research in formulating their hypotheses. The search engines *www.google.com* and *www.alta vista.com* seem to be the best to use as they are linked to more sites than any other.

4. Datalogging

If your department is fortunate enough to possess class sets of these instruments, you will find them invaluable in practical sessions. Dataloggers are instruments that collect data via sensors that plug into them, and relay the data to a computer for analysis. They provide a way of accurately measuring varying parameters, and can be set to take several thousand measurements per second for transient changes (such as obtaining the acceleration due to gravity from a falling ball bearing) or changes that would be impractical to measure because of the time needed (for example, changes in weather conditions like temperature, light intensity etc. over a couple of weeks).

The sensors you will usually come into contact with will be those for pH, temperature, light, motion (called 'light gates') and possibly current and voltage. Other sensors, for example, pressure, oxygen content, force and so on are available as well.

The value in using datalogging is that the data collected can be sent to a computer in the science laboratory and immediately analysed. This will include drawing graphs of the data, manipulating the graphs and any other pictorial ways of displaying the results. The value of this is that students can concentrate on the science behind the experiment rather than be bogged down in manipulating a large amount of data. Parts of graphs can be analysed, reciprocal plots can be made at the touch of a button to identify inverse proportionality, and statistical analysis can be employed.

The two main types of datalogger and sensors you may find in schools are firstly the Philip Harris 'Blue Box' sensors, that have been around for many years, but have the disadvantage that they need calibration each time they are used, and secondly Data Harvest 'EasySense' and 'Sense and Control' dataloggers, which are probably the state-of-the-art machines. These have the advantage that no sensors need calibrating and that being small they can be transported out of the laboratory more easily for fieldwork measurements. Their disadvantage is that they tend to be expensive.

5. Using graph packages and spreadsheets

Students find the analysis of results tedious. In order to help them with this problem there are many graph-drawing packages available and of course, Microsoft Excel has that facility. It is important, however, that students need to be able to draw graphs well by hand – because they are assessed in written papers – but if you as the teacher are happy with their competence, then using graph packages is perfectly acceptable. This helps the students concentrate on the science and on the relationships between variables rather than getting bogged down in the paperwork and number crunching. Excel is also useful for the analysis of large amounts of data. A good example of this is an investigation to measure the heat given off by a fuel and to find out the relationship between the number of bonds in the molecule of the fuel and the heat given off per mole of fuel. For each fuel there is a complicated several-stage calculation that has to be done, and then several results for the same fuel have to be averaged. This has to be repeated for several fuels. I have now been able to get this investigation done completely in a couple of lessons by pooling the results from the whole class, putting the results on Excel, and by pressing a button end up with a completed graph.

6. Use of word processing packages

Many students nowadays wish to use word processors to produce work. The use of word processors is to be encouraged as it enables even poor writers to produce a well-presented document. This is especially important regarding coursework. You should not forget that spelling, punctuation and grammar are also assessed and if students are able to use a spell-checker, not only does this help their literacy skills, but it also helps them obtain more marks.

You and computers

Your main use of computers will be in the production of worksheets for your classes. It is a good idea to learn how to touch-type as this makes the job much easier. Do not forget simple sentence construction, a low reading age and a suitable font for your sheets. Other areas will include research on the Internet, and the use of spreadsheets, in order to store student data and even work out examination percentages. Microsoft Powerpoint will be useful if you are fortunate enough in your department to have an interactive white-board. You will then use your Powerpoint presentation as part of your lesson. You will also be required to keep a record of any ICT used with students, and their capabilities using it. There is a programme of study for ICT stating that certain things must be covered across the curriculum. Your science department may have signed up to some of the statements and so you will need to check what you are expected to cover. One last thing, as you get more organised as a teacher, you may wish to invest in a palmtop computer yourself. As well as acting as a diary, an organiser, a to-do list and a notebook, you can load it with Word and Excel files that you can work on at home, in school, or in any place at any time if there is no computer free.

What about the future?

There is no doubt that the use of computers will increase even further in schools. One exciting development is the use of portals to develop e-communities. A portal called Digital Brain has been introduced which is enabling students and teachers to communicate across communities consisting of secondary schools, feeder primary schools and tertiary and higher colleges linked to them. Each section has its own level of access password-protected and so staff are able to set tests online and receive instant feedback from students; their marks being percentaged instantly and loaded into a password-protected mark book. The URL of the site is listed in Chapter 11.

Summary

The information revolution has taken schools by storm, and looks as if it will still increase its influence on education in the twenty-first century. However, keep things in perspective. If using ICT helps, enhances or motivates the students, then it is probably worthwhile using it. However, if it is used simply as a gimmick, there is probably a much better resource that the students can use to learn from – you.

11

Useful Websites

These few websites represent a few of the many hundreds of sites dedicated to education. I suggest that you look these up, and also follow some of the links to other sites of equal interest.

General

http://www.standards.dfee.gov.uk/ Government site that contains the national curriculum schemes of work.

http://www.ofsted.gov.uk/ The main Ofsted site, useful for looking at schools inspections prior to applying for a job.

http://www.qca.org.uk/ The Qualifications and Curriculum Authority (QCA) main site for all aspects of the National Curriculum.

http://www.hse.gov.uk/hthdir/noframes/coshh/ Health and – Coshh regulations.

http://www.adprima.com/assertive.htm Assertive discipline site – information on all aspects of assertive discipline.

http://www.canteach.gov.uk/support/induction/cep/ Teachers support including career entry profile. Here you will find information on your induction year.

http://www.canteach.gov.uk/support/induction/cep/faq-career-entry.htm Career entry profile information.

http://www.ase.org.uk/ Association for Science Education – useful resources for all science teachers – one of the most useful science teacher organisations.

http://www.ldpride.net/learningstyles.MI.htm Information on multiple intelligences.

http://www.geocities.com/CapeCanaveral/Cockpit/8107/index.html Information on demonstration lessons

http://www.cleapss.org.uk Information on health and safety in schools.

http://eqi.org/ and *http://www.connected.org/learn/school.html* Two sites devoted to emotional intelligence.

http://www.etln.org.uk/page26.html Information on effective teaching.

http://www.eskimo.com/~user/kids.html Gifted and talented students' resources.

http://www.gmu.edu/gmu/personal/time.html Time management tips.

http://www.axcis.co.uk/, *http://www.schooljobs.org.uk/cgi-bin/schooljobs.storefront* and *http://www.qualityteacherrecruitment.co.uk/teachers.htm* Three sites for teacher recruitment.

Examination boards

You can download GCSE and Post-16 syllabuses from the following sites:

http://www.aqa.org.uk/

http://www.edexcel.org.uk/

http://www.ocr.org.uk/OCR/WebSite/docroot/index.jsp

http://www.wjec.co.uk/exams.html

Teacher resources

http://www.nbii.gov/education/ General biology resources.

http://teachers.net/ General resources for teachers.

http://www.pbs.org/teachersource/ and *http://chem.lapeer.org/* Links to lots of demonstrations and practicals – a wealth of ideas.

http://www.rsc.org/ The Royal Society of Chemistry site – general resources under the Education part.

http://www.iop.org/ The Institute of Physics site – general resources under the education part.

http://www.iob.org/ The Institute of Biology site – general resources under the education part.

http://naturalsciences.sdsu.edu/links.html Biology resources and links.

http://www.thecatalyst.org/ General chemistry resources.

http://www.ba.infn.it/www/didattica.html General physics resources.

http://www.alleyns.org.uk/other/xwords.htm and *http://www.sec.org.za/rcross.html* Science crosswords.

http://www.tomwilson.com/david/NC/keywords/Sc.html Science keywords and links to resources.

http://www.teach-nology.com/worksheets/science/ General science worksheets.

http://sciencespot.net/Pages/classwksts.html General science worksheets and links.

http://www.creative-chemistry.org.uk/ Chemistry worksheets and links.

http://www.dcsd.k12.co.us/secondary/hrhs/hrhsphysics/physicstopicws.html

http://www.vast.org/vip/WORKSHEE/HOME.HTM

http://qldscienceteachers.tripod.com/worksheets/junior/physics/ Physics worksheets and links.

http://www.cheltcoll.gloucs.sch.uk/depts/biology/bioworksheet.html

http://qldscienceteachers.tripod.com/worksheets/biology/cells/

http://qldscienceteachers.tripod.com/worksheets/junior/biology/

http://qldscienceteachers.tripod.com/worksheets/junior/biology/ Biology worksheets and links.

http://www.spolem.co.uk/worksheets/human.htm *http://www.spolem.co.uk/worksheets/AS.htm* Biology worksheets (for post-16).

Appendices

The following appendices provide exemplar materials that will be of use to the student teacher and those in their first years of teaching. Some, if desired, may be photocopied, provided that they are used solely within the establishment where the user is teaching. These pages are clearly marked.

Appendix:
1. Literacy, numeracy, ICT and SNSC
2. Lesson observation proforma
3. Classroom discipline plan
4. Formal referral exemplar
5. Pupil action plan
6. Exemplar letter of complaint to a parent
7. Exemplar letter of commendation to a parent
8. Exemplar letter regarding a science trip
9. Ideas for starter activities
10. Ideas for plenary activities
11. Investigative work at KS3 pupil level indicators
12. Lesson plan template (e.g. during an observed lesson)
13. Using the Internet
14. Exemplar Internet treasure hunt for a science club
15. Memo template
16. Exemplar science treasure hunt for a science club
17. Library slip
18. Permission to be out of a lesson slip
19. Ideas for 'egg race' activities for end-of-term activities or science clubs
20. Markbook page templates
21. Planner page template (five-lesson day)
22. Planner page template (six-lesson day)

Appendix 1
Literacy, Numeracy, ICT and SMSC

Ideal lessons should contain other aspects as well as the science content covered by a three-part-lesson. The four main areas include:

▶ Literacy covering skills, use and knowledge of language.
▶ Numeracy covering skills, use and knowledge of number.
▶ ICT covering aspects of information and communications technology.
▶ SMSC covering knowledge and appreciation of spiritual, moral, social and cultural matters.

The following lists suggest ten key points for each of the above areas. An ideal lesson may include some of the following elements:

Literacy
1. Asking questions.
2. Giving elaborated answers as a result of open-ended questions.
3. Talking and listening to peers in pairs and group-work.
4. Giving a presentation to the whole class.
5. Reading from a range of different types of texts of appropriate difficulty.
6. Talking about the ideas in the texts.
7. Finding, collecting and organising information obtained from the texts.
8. Writing in a range of different forms.
9. Using spelling, punctuation and grammar accurately and creatively.
10. Writing fiction and non-fiction.

Numeracy
1. Solving problems and interpreting and checking results.
2. Using correct mathematical terms and vocabulary.
3. Showing appropriate degrees of accuracy in measurement.
4. Recalling number facts and manipulating whole numbers, fractions, decimals and percentages.
5. Using appropriate methods to calculate answers or results.
6. Substituting numbers into formulae.
7. Giving appropriate units of measurement in answers.
8. Making use of information presented in tables, charts, diagrams and graphs.
9. Representing data in pictures and graphs.
10. Analysing data and make predictions.

ICT
1. Using a search engine and the Internet to find information.
2. Identifying what information is relevant to a task and the suitability of content and style.
3. Using software to represent data in simple graphs, charts and tables.
4. Being able to justify the choice of presentation of data.
5. Using templates and master pages to increase efficiency of their reports.
6. Using software to investigate a model.
7. Using a spreadsheet and predicting the effects of changing a variable.
8. Planning and designing a presentation in digital media (e.g. Powerpoint).
9. Using e-mail securely and efficiently for messaging and supporting materials.
10. Using dataloggers and sensors accurately and correctly.

SMSC (Spiritual, Moral, Social and Cultural)
1. Understanding pattern and the order of creation of the universe.
2. Experiencing a sense of awe and wonder at the universe.
3. Having an awareness of their own and others' beliefs about the purpose of life.
4. Demonstrating and understanding the differences between right and wrong.
5. Developing relationships based on mutual trust and respect.
6. Working well together as a team (either in pairs or small groups).
7. Working together as a group to obtain whole-group rewards.
8. Understanding other cultures and lifestyles.
9. Understanding the contributions made to the field of science by people from other cultures (e.g. the Arabic people naming the stars).
10. Developing cross-cultural sensitivity.

Appendix 2
Lesson observation proforma

This document may be of use when observing peer lessons or observation of lessons by experienced teachers.

Lesson observation proforma

Date: .... Teacher: .... Observer: ....

Subject: .... Time: .... Year Group: ....

Teaching Set: .... Number present: ...... Boys: .... Girls: ....

No. of students on(a) SEN register: ..... (b) Gifted and talented register: ......

How was good discipline achieved?
- ▶
- ▶
- ▶
- ▶
- ▶

What was good about the starter activity and what ideas can I use for my starter activities, if any?
- ▶
- ▶
- ▶
- ▶
- ▶

What was good about the main activity and what ideas can I use, if any?
- ▶
- ▶
- ▶
- ▶

What was good about the plenary activity and what ideas can I use, if any?
- ▶
- ▶
- ▶
- ▶
- ▶

Any other aspects of the lesson which could be useful to try in my lessons for example, useful links to literacy, numeracy, ICT and SMSC?
- ▶
- ▶
- ▶
- ▶
- ▶

This sheet may be photocopied

Appendix 3
Typical classroom discipline plan

Classroom Discipline Plan

Teacher:._____

EXPECTATIONS
▶ Follow the teacher's instructions.
▶ Respect others in the room.
▶ Follow the lab safety rules at all times.

REWARDS
▶ Verbal praise.
▶ House point (and raffle ticket).
▶ Homework pass.
▶ Commendation.
▶ Group points leading to a whole class reward.

CONSEQUENCES
If you *choose not* to accept the learning skills set out above:
▶ Level 1: A warning.
▶ Level 2: Move to a new place to work on your own.
▶ Level 3: Detention for up to 5 minutes after the lesson.
▶ Level 4: Science detention and behaviour logged on an incident sheet.
▶ Level 5: Referral to a senior member of staff and parents informed.

This sheet may be photocopied

Appendix 4
A typical formal referral

Formal Referral

Student name.............................. Tutor/Teaching group ....

Date of incident........................... Lesson ....

Member of staff reporting incident...

Summary of the incident

....

....

....

....

....

....

....

....

....

....

Sanctions used by staff member/department:

....

....

Should there be parental involvement at this stage? (Y/N)...........................

This sheet may be photocopied

Appendix 5
Pupil action plan

Pupils who have been referred to a senior member of staff may, at the senior teacher's discretion, be placed on a report. The following proforma can be used to emphasise the type of behaviour modification necessary in order to satisfy the teacher concerned. In this way, the student (and parent) are clear about what is required and by when modification is necessary. Students should ensure that this is kept with them at all times. A copy should be kept by the teacher.

Pupil Action Plan

TARGET	Your target	Date set	Target review date	Achieved?
Enter the room sensibly				
Concentrate from the start of the lesson				
Do not talk when the teacher is talking				
Bring the correct equipment				
Follow instructions				
Stay on the task set				
Do not move around the room unnecessarily				
Do not interfere with others' equipment				
Write down all homework				
Hand homework in on time				
Accept punishment				
Accept criticism				
Display good manners				
Other targets				

This action plan has been agreed with   .... (Teacher)

.... (Pupil)

I have seen this action plan and I will support my child in reaching the targets set.

.... (Parent)

This sheet may be photocopied

Appendix 6
Letter of complaint to a parent

This is a typical letter of complaint from a classroom teacher to a parent. Ensure, however, that you have the correct surname for the parent or parents concerned.

Dear Mrs.............

I regret to inform you that your child David was involved in an incident in my lesson yesterday.

Here you have informed the parent that there was an incident, the time and date.

Despite warnings, and progression through my classroom discipline plan (a copy of which you can find in David's exercise book), he chose not to conform to the standard of behaviour I accept.

He persistently interfered with other students' experiments, and eventually his rudeness towards me resulted in him being removed from the class by the deputy headteacher after he reached Level 5 on my discipline plan.

I have consulted the head of department who will be placing David in the Science detention class on Tuesday evening after

*In these three paragraphs you have made the parent aware that David **knows** what is expected of him (he has the discipline plan in his book), and his mother can also refer to this. You have given details of the incident and why it is contrary to your discipline plan. You have also outlined the consequences.*

school for one hour. A copy of this letter will be placed in David's school file for reference should further action be necessary in the future.

I hope that I have your support in this matter and that you will discuss this incident with David as soon as possible.

Here you are asking for the parent's support (a good thing to have!) and you have shown yourself to be reasonable by being willing to discuss the situation if the parent wishes.

If you would like any further details of the incident, or you would like to discuss any aspect of David's attitude and progress in science please do not hesitate to contact me via the school office.

Yours sincerely

....
Science teacher, 10 set 2

Appendix 7
Letter of commendation to a parent

It is important that parents are made fully aware of how their children are progressing. An excellent way to motivate a student is by a commendation, either as a simple certificate or as a letter home to his or her parents. Writing letters home need not be an onerous task a standardised letter such as the one below can be kept on file and the student's name and reason for the commendation can be inserted individually.

Dear Mr..............

Letter of commendation

I teach Sally science in year 9 set 3. Last week the whole group was given a research task on the solar system as homework.

On receiving Sally's work I was exceptionally pleased with both its content and the standard at which Sally is working. She put a great deal of effort into the project over

> *Here you have made clear to the parent* **why** *you are pleased with his daughter.*

and above that which would normally be expected by a girl of her age. She deserves to be congratulated, hence my letter to you.

As a reward, Sally has been given a homework pass this week together with five house-points that will be counted towards a whole class reward at the end of term. Therefore Sally will have no science homework this week.

Perhaps you might like to look over Sally's project and add your own congratulations along with mine.

> *In the final sentences you have explained what rewards you will give Sally, and also subtly invite the parents to reward her at home as well. In this way students may realse that a commendation letter will have knock-on effects!*

Yours sincerely

....
Science teacher year 9 set 3

Appendix 8
Letter to a parent regarding a science trip

Dear Parents

Proposed trip to the Science Museum, London on 14th May

As part of the year 10 science course, we are proposing to offer all students the opportunity of a trip to the Science Museum in London on 14th May. This has been

> *The first paragraph details why the trip is necessary and how the students will benefit from it. It's not just a day out.*

approved by the head and governors and will be a valuable experience for the students in preparation for their year 10 examinations in June. They will be completing several worksheets whilst at the museum, and will also be expected to undertake some follow-up work when back at school.

We have arranged transport by coach that will be leaving school at 9.00 am prompt on 14th May. We shall be returning by 4.00 pm so that your child can catch the

> *In this paragraph you have given all the details of the trip, and what you expect from the students – an important point if there is a problem. Students need to* **know exactly where they stand.**

normal school bus home. Your child will need to bring a packed lunch, writing equipment, a supply of paper or an exercise book and a waterproof coat in the event of inclement weather. Cameras, personal stereos and mobile phones will be allowed (the latter for emergency use only) but the school cannot be held responsible for damage or loss. We expect the students to be on their best behaviour and to turn up in full uniform. We hope to have at least five full hours at the museum.

The cost of the trip, which is heavily subsidised by the science department, will be £4.50 mostly to cover coach travel to and from the museum and reprographic costs. Cheques should be made payable to the school, and at-

> *Finally – the cost. It is always important to allow parents on low income to feel that their child will not miss out if they cannot pay the full amount required. Discussion with the head of department may result in reduced cost, or payment buy instalments or the cost waived altogether.*

tached to the parental consent slip. If the cost of the trip presents a problem to you, please let me know in confidence.

I look forward to hearing from you.

Yours sincerely

....
Science Teacher year 10

Appendix 9
Ideas for starter activities in the KS3 3-part lesson

Always *plan* to use a starter activity while ensuring that any starter contributes to the overall lesson objective. Every starter should be clear, concise and focused. The following list suggests some good starters:

- **Card sort** – matching definitions/grouping 'like' terms, e.g. mammals.

- **Guess the mystery object** – the teacher describes and pupils work out what it is from the clues.

- **Bingo** – students have prepared bingo cards and cover up the areas with counters, for example, when they hear the correct definition of a scientific keyword.

- **Word association** – using concepts to generate thoughts. This is effective when revising a topic. Select a topic and a concept, see how many links can be made – the teacher puts them into a 'mindmap' on the board.

- **Guess the word or definition** in 20 questions or less – in pairs, using only 'yes' or 'no'.

- **Explain or demonstrate** the correct use of a piece of equipment.

- **Countdown** conundrum – keyword to work out – this is a good use of literacy in science.

- **Choose a topic** and give five minutes to add everything they know (in pairs).

- **Choose five things** learnt last lesson – and rank them in order of importance.

- **Time out** – give your pupils a minute or two to reflect on their learning last lesson and talk about it with a neighbour.

- **True/false cards** – use answers on cards held high with 'yes' or 'no', 'true' or 'false' / red, yellow or green cards (don't know/think I know/sure I know) to give the teacher instant feedback to any questions asked.

- **What is the question?** – students are given an 'answer' and have to provide an appropriate question.

- **Ask the teacher** – students are invited to ask the teacher five really challenging things that they would like to know about the topic for that lesson.

▶ **Lists** e.g. 'List five advantages and/or disadvantages...'.

▶ **Arguments** – give the class or groups a theory and five minutes to come up with one argument that supports it and one that does not. Then discuss them.

▶ **Odd-one-out** – from a pile, choose certain cards that relate to each other leaving an odd one out

▶ **Just a minute** (well, at least half a minute!) – challenge members of the class to talk for half a minute on the topic of the lesson. They may repeat the keyword/topic as often as they like, but must speak without repetition, hesitation or deviation.

Appendix 10
Ideas for plenary activities in the KS3 3-part lesson

In the plenary activity the bulk of the consolidation of the learning done in the lesson takes place. Plenaries are of great importance, therefore, in raising achievement and in ensuring that students learn. Some ideas of good plenaries are listed below:

- **Call my bluff** – Students write three definitions for a key word, one correct and two wrong they then test each other.

- **Lucky dip** – Pick a key word written on paper from a box at random and explain/describe/define the word.

- **True or false** – Ten quick fire questions on the topic.

- **Real life** – List three ways what you have learned can be used in real life/other lessons.

- **List** three things you or your neighbour has learned today.

- **List** five things that you know now about the lesson's topic that you did not know before.

- **Summarise** a topic in five sentences, then five words, then one word.

- **Top Tips** – List five top tips that you would recommend someone knowing if they were to understand this topic well

- **Write a paragraph** 'What have you learned today?'

- **Exemplars** – Pupils identify three good/bad things about someone else's work (make sure that the work is anonymous!).

- **Yes/no answers** – Answer questions without using 'yes',' no' or key words.

- **Concept loops** – A question and an answer to a question on another card are written on each card. Pupils have to find the pupil with the answer to their own question in the class and stand next to them until the class forms a circle – good for bodily kinaesthetic learners.

- **Make a science dictionary** – Students complete definitions/key words as they are learned making up a dictionary/glossary of science words e.g. in the backs of their exercise books.

- **Complete a crossword** or a word search.

▶ **Pupil feedback** – Pupils work on different aspects of a topic and teach each other.

▶ **Representatives** – Pupils travel to other groups to gain information and report back.

▶ **Mnemonics** – Create mnemonics of subject-specific vocabulary used in the lesson.

▶ **Flowchart** – Construct a flowchart – summarise the lesson in steps/flowchart.

▶ **Write a book jacket** – Write a short blurb about a lesson topic.

▶ **A rap** – Produce a 4–8 line rap or poem about what has been learned during the lesson.

Appendix 11
What students need to know regarding investigative work at KS3

These checklists give students an idea of what they need to achieve in investigative work to be given the appropriate level. They could be either given to the students individually, or enlarged and displayed on the wall of the laboratory.

Level 4 – Investigative work
▶ You recognise that scientific ideas are based on evidence.

▶ In your own investigative work, you decide on an appropriate approach to answer a question.

▶ Where appropriate, you describe, or show in the way you perform your task, how to vary one factor while keeping others the same.

▶ Where appropriate, you make predictions.

▶ You select information from sources provided for them.

▶ You select suitable equipment and make a series of observations and measurements that are adequate for the task.

▶ You record your observations, comparisons and measurements using tables and bar charts.

▶ You begin to plot points to form simple graphs, and use these graphs to point out and interpret patterns in your data.

▶ You begin to relate your conclusions to these patterns and to scientific knowledge and understanding, and to communicate them with appropriate scientific language.

▶ You suggest improvements in your work, giving reasons.

Level 5 – Investigative work
▶ You describe how experimental evidence and creative thinking have been combined to provide a scientific explanation.

▶ When you try to answer a scientific question, you identify an appropriate approach.

▶ You select from a range of sources of information. When the investigation involves a fair test, you identify key factors to be considered.

▶ Where appropriate, you make predictions based on your scientific knowledge and understanding.

▶ You select apparatus for a range of tasks and plan to use it effectively.

▶ You make a series of observations, comparisons or measurements with precision appropriate to the task.

▶ You begin to repeat observations and measurements and to offer simple explanations for any differences you encounter.

▶ You record observations and measurements systematically and, where appropriate, present data as line graphs.

▶ You draw conclusions that are consistent with the evidence and begin to relate these to scientific knowledge and understanding.

▶ You make practical suggestions about how your working methods could be improved.

▶ You use appropriate scientific language and conventions to communicate quantitative and qualitative data.

Level 6 – Investigative work

▶ You describe evidence for some accepted scientific ideas and explain how the interpretation of evidence by scientists leads to the development and acceptance of new ideas.

▶ In your own investigative work, you use scientific knowledge and understanding to identify an appropriate approach.

▶ You select and use sources of information effectively.

▶ You make enough measurements, comparisons and observations for the task.

▶ You measure a variety of quantities with precision, using instruments with fine-scale divisions.

▶ You choose scales for graphs and diagrams that enable them to show data and features effectively.

▶ You identify measurements and observations that do not fit the main pattern shown.

▶ You draw conclusions that are consistent with the evidence and use scientific knowledge and understanding to explain them.

▶ You make reasoned suggestions about how your working methods could be improved.

▶ You select and use appropriate methods for communicating qualitative and quantitative data using scientific language and conventions.

Level 7 – Investigative work

▶ You describe some predictions based on scientific theories and give examples of the evidence collected to test these predictions.

▶ In your own work, you use scientific knowledge and understanding to decide on appropriate approaches to questions.

▶ You identify the key factors in complex contexts and in contexts in which variables cannot readily be controlled, and plan appropriate procedures.

▶ You synthesise information from a range of sources, and identify possible limitations in secondary data.

▶ You make systematic observations and measurements with precision, using a wide range of apparatus.

▶ You identify when you need to repeat measurements, comparisons and observations in order to obtain reliable data.

▶ Where appropriate, you represent data in graphs, using lines of best fit.

▶ You draw conclusions that are consistent with the evidence and explain these using scientific knowledge and understanding.

▶ You begin to consider whether the data you have collected is sufficient for your conclusions.

▶ You communicate what you have done using a wide range of scientific and technical language and conventions, including symbols and flow diagrams.

Appendix 12
Lesson plan example for use when being observed

Example given is for an introductory lesson on hydrogen. Each lesson plan should include the features below, plus, if possible, some indications of use of numeracy, literacy, ICT, SMSC and preferred learning styles.

Science lesson plan

Date: _____ Teacher:_____ Observer:_____
Subject: _____ Time: _____ Year group:_____
Teaching Set: _____ Number present:_____ Boys: ___   Girls:___

No. of students on (a) SEN register:____ (b) Gifted and talented register: ____

Learning objectives
Know how metals react with acids.
Know how to test for hydrogen.

Approximate level: 5.

Mental warm-up/engagement activity
Question and answer session to ascertain pupils' prior knowledge of acids.
Quick demonstration of how to conduct the experiment safely.

Main activity and classroom organisation
Production of hydrogen using zinc and hydrochloric acid using a thistle funnel/conical flask arrangement. Collect any hydrogen produced and test for it by holding a lighted splint at arms length at the mouth of the tube. The characteristic 'pop' suggests hydrogen present. Extension activity to include testing other metals and acids if there is time.

Resources
Conical flask, thistle funnel, delivery tube, trough, test tubes. Use of Bunsen Burner, splints. Selection of metals (zinc, iron, magnesium, copper) and acids (hydrochloric, sulphuric).
Hodder Science A pages 130–131.

Differentiation
More able (including G and T):
Enrichment by testing other metals and acids to discover whether or not all metals produce hydrogen with acids.
Less able:
Ensure that least able manage to test for hydrogen (with help if necessary) using zinc and hydrochloric acid.

Plenary
Question and Answer session on the reactions of metals and an acid. Complete 'Remember' exercise in Hodder Science A – page 131.

Risk assessment and safety issues
Acids are corrosive wear goggles. Hydrogen is flammable.

Homework
Complete Homework sheet A5 by next lesson.

Appendix 13
Using the Internet as a research tool

Using the Internet

You will need to research the answers to as many of the following challenges using the Internet. Each correct answer will gain you a point.

Search engines that you can use include:

www.google.com (probably the most useful)
www.altavista.com
www.lycos.com
www.ask.com (the 'Ask Jeeves' site)

Using a search engine
1. Type any key words into the search box and press return. The new page will display sites that may be relevant.
2. You can narrow your search by using the search engine in a clever way. Suppose you are looking for pages on organs in the human body. If you type

ORGANS IN THE HUMAN BODY

you will get pages on the human body as well as pages on the musical instrument - the organ. To avoid this you can type

HUMAN + BODY + ORGAN − MUSICAL INSTRUMENT

Now you will only get pages that you need. Because of the ' + ' signs you will only get pages that have references to 'human' AND 'body' AND 'organs. Because of the ' − ' sign in front of 'musical instrument' you will not get any pages with the word 'organ' used as an instrument.

Another way to search smartly is to put a particular phrase in speech marks. If you are looking for the year in which Isaac Newton died, you can enter the words

'ISAAC NEWTON DIED IN'

enclosed in speech marks as shown, and any page containing this phrase will show up. The chances are that the year will then be given to complete the phrase.

Don't forget – some of the research topics are easy – some are difficult to find, and others are almost impossible.

Good luck!

This page may be photocopied

Appendix 14
Exemplar Internet treasure hunt for a science club

Name:.. Tutor group. ....

Find the answers to these questions using the Internet

1. What is the diameter of Mars? ....

2. What is a Pulsar? ....

3. When was Isaac Newton born? ....

4. Who was the first woman in space? ....

5. Who was the third human to set foot on the moon? ....

6. Which metal is used, apart from stainless steel, in making artificial hip joints?
   ....

7. Who discovered the gas helium? ....

8. In an atomic clock, at what frequency does a caesium atom vibrate? ....

9. How many times brighter is a full moon than a half moon? ....

10. The words *rhythm* and *syzygy* are the longest in the English Language that have no vowels. Everyone knows what rhythm is, but what is a syzygy? ....
    ....

11. What is the name of the world's largest chemical company?....................
    ....

12. February 1865 was the only month in recorded history that something did not happen in the sky. What was it? ....

13. How long is a jiffy?..

14. What is the international phone code for Antarctica?............................

15. In which year was stainless steel invented? ....

16. What is the densest substance on earth?..

17. What radioactive isotope is used in smoke detectors?............................

18. A millisecond is $^1/1,000$ second, and a microsecond is $^1/1,000,000$ second, but what is the name given to the smallest unit of time?................................

This page may be photocopied

99

19. When Neil Armstrong went to the moon, how much fuel did the Saturn V rocket consume each second? ....

20. How many pairs of legs does a krill shrimp have? ....

21. What shape is the pupil of an octopus's eye?...

22. The Russian composer, Alexander Borodin, wrote many works including an opera called *Prince Igor*. However, his main job was in science. What did he do? ....

23. What chemical do onions and garlic contain that gives them their characteristic smell?...

24. Which is the only letter that does not appear anywhere in the periodic table?

    ....

25. Which weighs more – a pound of feathers or a pound of gold? Be careful – this one may catch you out!...

This page may be photocopied

Internet Treasure Hunt 2003 - Answers

1. 6780 km.
2. A revolving neutron star producing regular pulses of radiation.
3. Christmas Day 1642.
4. Valentina Tereshkova.
5. Pete Conrad (Apollo 12).
6. Titanium.
7. William Ramsay.
8. 9,192,631,770.
9. 9.
10. When three astronomical bodies line up.
11. Du Pont.
12. There was no full moon.
13. $^1/_{100}$ second.
14. 672.
15. 1913.
16. The metal osmium.
17. Americium-241.
18. A yoctosecond (0.000000000000000000000001 second).
19. 15 tons.
20. 11.
21. Rectangular.
22. He was professor of chemistry at Moscow university.
23. Sulphur.
24. The letter J.
25. The answer is not that they weigh the same. A pound of feathers weighs far more than a pound of gold. Feathers are weighed on the avoirdupois scale where there are 16 ounces to the pound. Gold, silver, platinum and other precious metals are weighed on the troy scale where there are only 12 ounces to the pound.

This page may be photocopied

Appendix 15
Exemplar memo template

Memo

From:...   To:...

Date: ....   Subject: ....

....
....
....
....
....
....
....
....
....
....
....
....
....
....

Reply:

....

....

....

This page may be photocopied

Appendix 16
Exemplar science treasure hunt for a science club

Treasure hunt............................ Name..

You will be working as *teams* to complete as many of the tasks in this list as possible, in the time given to you. You will *each* get a point for every task your *team* completes. You might decide to share around the tasks in your team to try to get as many completed in the time available so that you ALL get points.

Don't forget – some tasks are easy, some are difficult – and some are nearly impossible.

Tasks:

1. Find out the height of the school tower... m

2. Make a leaf rubbing of a leaf from a **sycamore** tree. (on the paper provided).

3. Find a piece of **limestone** and show it to the teacher.

4. Measure the pH of the soil in the school copse pH.................................

5. What is the metal in the railings leading up to the Music room?...............

6. Count the number of legs on a woodlouse ....

7. Make a bark rubbing of an **oak** tree (on the paper provided).

8. Find out what Jocelyn Bell Burnell is famous for ....

9. Find a bird's **feather**. Stick it in the space with sticky tape.

10. Find and identify two **white flowers** in the school grounds

    (a) .... (b) ....

11. Find a **four-leaf clover**. Stick it in the space with sticky tape.

12. Find five **crisp bags** and present them to your teacher.......... [tick if done]

13. Find out the colours of three different **waste bins** (three different colours)

14. Find out what is represented in the **Hertzsprung-Russell** diagram.............

    ....

15. Complete the **cross-number**

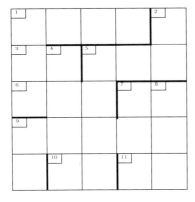

Clues across
  1. Next year.
  3. Number of weeks in a year.
  5. 12 × 12.
  6. James Bond ....
  7. pH of the strongest alkali possible
  9. 24 × 1000 then add 86
  10. Number of degrees in a right angle take away the number of toes on 2 feet.
  11. 17 × 4.

Clues down
  1. Number of fingers on one hand × the date of Christmas Day X number of hands.
  2. Number of days of the week × number of months in the year.
  4. 2 × 2 × 2 × 2 .... 11 times.
  5. Number of minutes in an hour × number of seconds in a minute + 2, then take away 100.
  7. Number of degrees in a triangle + number of legs on an insect.
  8. 234 × 2.
  9. All the fingers and toes + 3.

This page may be photocopied

16. Find a shell (for example – a snail shell).

17. Find a pine cone.

18. Complete the word search. The answers are all chemical elements.

M	U	I	L	E	H
U	U	P	E	N	D
I	O	I	A	O	L
D	T	A	D	E	O
O	S	T	I	N	G
S	S	I	U	M	I

Words: SODIUM TIN
HELIUM GOLD
LEAD NEON
INDIUM

The letters that are left spell out another element. What is it? ....

This page may be photocopied

Appendices 17 and 18
Exemplar library and permission slips

Library

Pupil's name............................. Tutor/teaching group...................

Date....................................... Lesson ....

The above pupil has permission to use the library for the purposes of:

....

Signed

....

Permission to be out of a lesson

Pupil's name............................. Tutor/teaching group...................

Date....................................... Lesson ....

The above pupil has permission to be out of this lesson.

Reason ....

....

Signed

....

This page may be photocopied

Appendix 19
Ideas for 'egg race' activities for end-of-term activities or science clubs

'Egg race' activities

'Egg races' are so called because they originally were problem solving activities associated with the transportation of an egg between two points in the shortest time, by using only an agreed selection of materials and power source. Now the name has been transferred to any activity requiring logical problem solving to reach a solution to a problem set. Egg races are excellent activities to use either in the main bulk of teaching or as an end of term activity. They need to be kept as simple as possible but very open-ended. They all need to have the following parameters:

1. Group work
The use of groups is of paramount importance. Co-operation in groups to arrive at a solution develops interdependence and trust. Try to make each group approximately the same size and of mixed ability.

2. Rules
Everyone needs to know the rules and the constraints within which they are working. If only a certain material is allowed then stick to the rule. Consequently the rules need to be simple so that everyone knows them by heart.

3. Incentive
Although well-motivated pupils will do well in this activity whatever the incentive, it is always more fun to provide a prize to the winning group. This may be anything from house points to something more tangible such as a chocolate bar or even a book token (if the budget can stretch to it).

4. Testing
The test for the winner has to be seen to be fair and accurate. Simple measurement of length, height, mass etc. are easy to achieve, and the winner can be chosen with little argument. Interim testing by the pupils to check their own progress can be arranged if so desired.

5. Prior knowledge

Pupils need to have some prior knowledge before tackling the problem. For example, the strength inherent in triangular structures (as is evident in bridges and towers such as the Eiffel Tower) needs to be discussed before building the structure.

6. Planning

Insist that there is a planning stage (10–30 mins depending upon the total time available and the activity) where there is to be no actual building. The groups need to plan their solution to the problem on paper (or by using a computer draw facility) and then, after arriving at the final solution, stick to it as it is being built. This ensures that the pupils work the problem themselves, and do not merely copy another group as they see their structure taking shape.

7. Time limit

There should be a time limit on the activity (again depending on the total time available and the actual activity – from 30 mins to 1 hour). This needs to be adhered to, in order that the whole activity is seen to be fair. 10 minute warnings and 5 minute warnings can be given!

Suggested activities

1. Tallest tower

Provide pupils with: A3 piece of thin card or paper, ruler, scissors, 2 metres of sticky tape wound onto a plastic cotton reel (to prevent it sticking).

Task: Build the tallest free-standing structure possible using only the paper/card and sticky tape provided. The structure must be able to be transported to a table for testing and must stand freely. The tallest structure on testing will win.

Hints: Triangular cross sections are usually the strongest. Steer the pupils into an open-lattice structure based on triangular cross-section straws (like the Eiffel tower) made from card cut and folded. The author once did this with older pupils and one group, making exceptionally thin triangular cross-section straws cut from an A4 sheet of card and produced a structure that was over 2 metres tall from the ground. Don't forget that the lower regions of the tower need to be the strongest to support the upper parts. Failure to do this will result in the tower collapsing under its own weight when the pupils near the end of the activity. This causes much amusement to the other groups, but it is a disaster to the group to which it happens!

2. Strongest bridge

Provide pupils with: A3 piece of thin card or paper, ruler, scissors, 2 metres of sticky tape wound onto a plastic cotton reel (to prevent it sticking).

Task: To build a bridge between two supports (say the edges of two tables) spaced 30 cm apart (the bridge will, therefore have to be longer than this so that it overlaps the edge). Only the materials provided may be used, and the bridge will have to be transported to the tables for testing so it cannot be fixed to the table. The bridge supporting the most weight on testing will be the winner.

Hints: Again, persuade the pupils to use triangular cross-sections or at least corrugation to achieve strength. At the end the bridge should be tested to destruction by suspending masses on it using a mass holder and bent coat hanger placed at the centre of the bridge hanging down. Add weights progressively until the bridge starts to collapse, or slips between the two tables because it bends too much.

3. Stock cube
Provide pupils with: a stock cube, an A3 piece of card, a balloon, 2 straws, 2 metres of sticky tape wound on a cotton reel.

Task: Using only the materials provided make a vehicle that will transport a stock cube along a 5 m line of string held taut across the classroom. The vehicle that travels furthest is the winner, but in the event of two or more vehicles reaching the 5m line, the fastest vehicle will be deemed the winner.

Hints: This challenge is one where the groups can explore the aerodynamics of a balloon rocket. The winner will be the team that manages to use the balloon as a rocket, stabilised with wings of card and kept on track with the straw threaded through the 5 m line of string. Make sure, however, that the children know the rules. The author once did this with a particularly bright set of youngsters, who, after reading the rules (which omitted the string) promptly cut the balloon into strips of rubber and used them to catapult the stock cube, not only across the room but out of the window into the playground. Although they scored little for adhering to the spirit of the rules, they scored full marks for lateral thinking!

4. Longest cantilever out from a desk
Provide pupils with: A3 piece of thin card or paper, ruler, scissors, 2 metres of sticky tape wound onto a plastic cotton reel (to prevent it sticking).

Task: Build the longest free-standing structure possible using only the paper/card and sticky tape provided, that sticks out from a table. The structure must be able to be transported to a table for testing and must stand freely. The longest reach out from the desk on testing will win.

Hints: This is a challenging task as it combines the need for the most mass to be concentrated on the desk, coupled with the need for a long reach and strength in the structure protruding from the desk. The commonest mistakes made will be the lack of mass at the end on the table, making the structure topple.

5. Spaghetti structure
Provide pupils with: 100 pieces of spaghetti, 2 metres of sticky tape wound onto a plastic cotton reel (to prevent it sticking).

Task: Build the tallest free-standing structure possible using only the spaghetti and sticky tape provided. The structure must be able to be transported to a table for testing and must stand freely. The tallest structure on testing will win.

Hints: This is a very similar exercise to number 1, but in this case triangular cross sections are impractical. Make the pupils aware that uncooked spaghetti has a very low lateral strength (sticks can be broken very easily if bent) but a very high tensile strength (pulling a stick will not break it). They should be able to incorporate these ideas into their design.

6. Wind propelled vehicle
Provide pupils with: A3 piece of thin card or paper, ruler, scissors, 2 metres of sticky tape wound onto a plastic cotton reel (to prevent it sticking), 4 cocktail sticks, A3 piece of tissue paper, 6 straws, a piece of modelling clay the size of a walnut. Access to a table fan.

Task: To make a vehicle that will be propelled using wind power alone. The winning vehicle will be the first to cover a 3 metre track (or in the event of no vehicle covering the track, the one that goes furthest). Only the materials supplied can be used.

Hints: Probably the hardest challenge, this requires advanced building skills. The pupils should aim to achieve a light structure, probably with three, not four, card wheels to cut down on friction, and a large sail made from the tissue paper. Cunning pupils may see the use of the cotton reel as a material, and use it as a heavy base for the sail to fit into. This is within the rules, as they are using something provided.

Appendix 20
Markbook page templates

CLASS.............. NAME	TUT. GP	KS2 SATs	CATs score	Reading Test	Pref. Lg. St.	Tgt. Min. Lev.														

This page may be photocopied

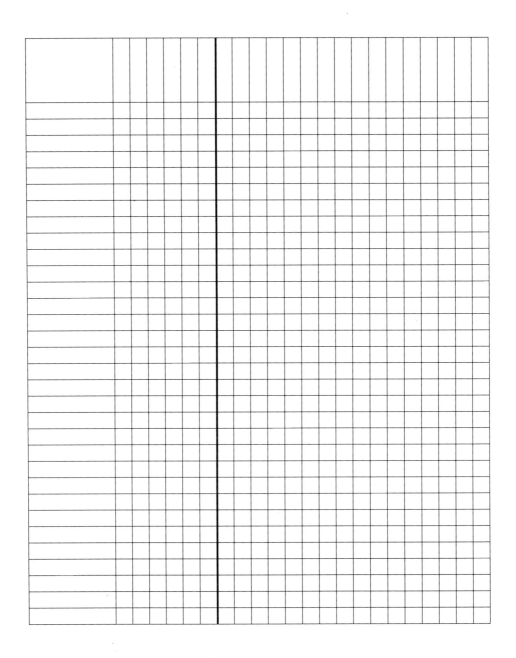

This page may be photocopied

Appendix 21
Planner page template (six-lesson day)

Day .... Date ....

Lesson	Class	Lesson planned	Homework
1			
2			
3			
4			
5			

After school activities (e.g. meetings)

This page may be photocopied

Appendix 22
Planner page template (six-lesson day)

Day .... Date ....

Lesson	Class	Lesson planned	Homework
1			
2			
3			
4			
5			
6			

After school activities (e.g. meetings)

This page may be photocopied

Useful Addresses

England, Wales and Northen Ireland

ALAOME (Association of LEA Advisory Officers for Multicultural Education) Chris Vieler-Porter, Chair ALAOME Evaluation, Advisory and Curriculum Services, Education Centre, Queens Road, Walthamstow, London E17 8QS. Tel: 020 8509 4218. E-mail: Chris.Vieler-Porter@edu.lbwf.gov.uk

Associated Examining Board, Stag Hill House, Guildford, Surrey GU2 5XJ. Tel: 01483 506506. E-mail:aeb@aeb.org.uk

Association of Teachers and Lecturers (ATL), 7 Northumberland Street, London WC2N 5DA. Tel: 020 7930 6441. Fax: 020 7930 1359. E-mail: info@atl.org.uk

Association of University Teachers, Egmont House, 25–31 Tavistock Place, London WC1H 9UT. Tel: 020 7670 9700. Fax: 020 7670 9799. E-mail: hq@aut.org.uk

Awdurdod Cwricwlwm ac Asesu Cymru (ACAC)/Curriculum and Assessment Authority for Wales, Castle Buildings, Womanby Street, Cardiff CF1 9SX. Tel: 01222 344946.

The Basic Skills Agency, Commonwealth House, 1–19 New Oxford Street, London WC1A 1NU. Tel: 020 7405 4017. Fax: 020 7404 6626. E-mail: enquiries@basic-skills.co.uk Website: http://www.basic-skills.co.uk. Formerly: Adult Literacy and Basic Skills Unit (ALBSU).

BBC – Education Information, Unit G420, White City, 201 Wood Lane, London W12 7TS.

BBC Educational Publishing, PO Box 234, Wetherby, W. Yorks LS23 7EU. (Written enquiries only.) Address for free cassettes of missed school radio programmes.

Bilingual Supplies for Children, PO Box 4081, Bournemouth BH8 9YX. Tel/fax: 01202 246837. Website: http://www.bilingual-supplies.co.uk Titles for French, German, Spanish, Italian, Chinese and Vietnamese.

Bilingualism, Languages, Literacies and Education Network (BLEN), 35 Connaught Road, London N4 4NT. Tel/fax: 020 7281 8686. E-mail: blened@rmplc.co.uk Website: http://www.blen.org.uk/ A non-profit making, independent, teacher friendly forum for bilingualism, languages, literacies and education forum.

Bolton. The Multicultural Resource Centre and Multicultural Books, POBox 298, The Moss C.P. School, Falkirk Drive, Breightmet, Bolton BL2 6FU. Tel/fax: 01204 366 868. Multi-lingual posters, maps and friezes.

Bristol Education Centre, Sheridan Road, Horfield, Bristol BS7 0PU. Tel: 0117 9311111.

The British Council, Information Centre, Fifth Floor, Bridgewater House, 58 Whitworth Street, Manchester M1 6BB. Tel: 0161 957 7755. Fax: 0161 957 7762. E-mail (course enquiries): education.enquiries@britcoun.org E-mail (other ELT enquiries): general.enquiries@britcoun.org Website: http://www.britcoun.org/ English overseas and overseas students in the UK. Information about teaching English as a foreign language.

British Educational Communications and Technology Agency (BECTa), Milburn Hill Road, Science Park, Coventry CV4 7JJ. Tel: 024 7641 6994. Fax: 024 7641 1418. E-mail: Becta@becta.org.uk Website: http://www.becta.org.uk ESOL website: http://www.becta.org.uk/inclusion/esol/index.html

The British Library Newspaper Library, Colindale Ave, London NW9 5HE. Tel: 020 7412 7353.

Channel 4 Schools, PO Box 100, Warwick CV34 6TZ. Tel: 01926 433333.

City and Guilds, 1 Giltspur Street, London EC1A 9DD. Tel: 020 7294 2468. E-mail: enquiry@city-and-guilds.co.uk

Commission for Racial Equality (CRE), Elliot House, 10–12 Allington Street, London SW1E 5EH. Tel: 020 7828 7022. Fax: 020 7630 7605. Minicom: 020 7932 5419.

Commonwealth Institute, Commonwealth Resource Centre, Contact: Librarian Kensington High Street, London W8 6NQ. Tel: 020 7603 4535. Fax: 020 7603 2807 E-mail: crc@commonwealth.org.uk Website: http://www.commonwealth.org.uk

Confederation of Indian Organisations (UK) (CIO), Rajesh Kalhan, Director 5 Westminster Bridge Road, London SE1 7XW. Tel: 020 7928 9889. Fax: 020 7620 4025. E-mail: cio@gn.apc.org

Department for Education and Employment (DFEE), Sanctuary Buildings, Great Smith Street, London SW1P 3BT. Tel: 020 7925 5555. **DFEE Publications Centre**, PO Box 6927, London E3 3NZ. Tel: 020 7510 0150.

Department of Education for Northern Ireland (DENI), Rathgael House, Balloo Road, Bangor.

Europa Centre, The Walk, Hornchurch, Essex RM11 3TL. **U.K. Section (EAT)**, 20 Brookfield, Highgate West Hill, London N6 6AS. Tel: 020 8340 9136.

Eurotunnel Education Dept, St Martin's Plain, Cheriton High St, Folkestone, Kent CT19 4QD. Tel: 01303 270111.

General Teaching Council for England, 3rd Floor Cannon House, 24 The Priory, Queensway, Birmingham B4 6BS. Tel: 0870 001 0308

Graduate Teacher Training Registry, Fulton House, Jessop Avenue, Cheltenham, Gloucestershire GL50 3SH. Tel: 01242 544788.

Hounslow Language Service, Hounslow Education Centre, Martindale Road, Hounslow TW4 7HE. Tel: 020 8570 2392 (Primary). 020 8570 4186 (Secondary). Fax: 020 8570 9965. Publisher of EAL and bilingual support materials.

International Baccalaureate Organisation, Peterson House, Fortran Road, St Mellons, Cardiff CF3 0LT, Wales. Tel: 01222 774000. E-mail: ibca@ibo.org

League for Exchange of Commonwealth Teachers, Commonwealth House 7 Lion Yard, Tremadoc Road, Clapham, London SW4 7NQ. Tel: 020 7498 1101. Fax: 020 7720 5403.

Learning Design (Tower Hamlets), Tower Hamlets Professional Development Centre, English Street, London E3 4TA. Tel: 020 8983 1944. Fax: 020 8983 1932. E-mail: info@learningdesign.org Website: http://www.learningdesign.org

London Chamber of Commerce and Industry Examinations Board, Athena House, 112 Station Road, Sidcup, Kent DA15 7BJ. Tel: 020 8302 0261. Fax: 020 8302 4169/020 8309 5169. E-mail at: custserv@lccieb.org.uk

Mantra Publishing Ltd, 5 Alexandra Grove, London N12 8NU. Tel: 020 8445 5123. Fax: 020 8446 7745. E-mail: orders@mantrapublishing.com Website: http://www.mantrapublishing.com Bilingual readers in ethnic community languages and English.

Milet Publishing Ltd, 19 North End Parade, London W14 0SJ Tel: 020 7603 5477. Fax: 020 7610 5475. E-mail: info@milet.com Website: http://www.milet.com Materials in Turkish and dual language children's books in other community languages.

Minority Rights Group, Contact: Frances Smith 379 Brixton Road, London SW9 7DE. Tel: 020 7978 9498. Fax: 020 7738 6265. E-mail: minority.rights@mrgmail.org Website: http://www.minorityrights.org Some materials available for use in schools, especially dual-text booklets in main refugee languages.

Multilingual Community Rights Shop, 213 Camberwell Road, London, SE5 0HG. Tel: 020 7703 4442. Fax: 020 7703 8393. E-mail: multilingual@rightshop.swinternet.co.uk

Multilingual Matters Ltd, Frankfurt Lodge, Clevedon Hall, Victoria Road, Clevedon, North Somerset BS21 7HH. Tel: 01275 876 519. Fax: 01275 871 673. E-mail: info@multilingual-matters.com Website: http://www.multilingual-matters.com

Muslim Printers & Booksellers, 423 Stratford Road, Sparkhill, Birmingham B11 4LB. Tel: 0121 773 8301. Fax: 0121 773 1735.

Nant Gwrtheyrn, National Centre for Language and Culture, Nant Gwrtheyrn, Llithfaen, Pwllheli, Gwynedd, LL53 6PA. Tel: 01758 750 334. Fax: 01758 750 335. E-mail: post@nantgwr.com. Website: http://www.nantgwr.com

National Association for Language Development in the Curriculum (NALDIC), c/o Hugh South, South Herts LCSC, Tolpits Lane, Watford WD1 8NT. Tel: 01923 231 855. Fax: 01923 225 130. Website: http://www.naldic.org.uk/

National Association for Special Educational Needs (NASEN), House 4/5, Amber Business Village, Tamworth, Staffs B77 4RP. Tel: 01827 311500. E-mail: welcome@nasen.org.uk

National Association of Schoolmasters/Union of Women Teachers (NAS/ UWT), Hillscourt Education Centre, Rose Hill, Rednal, Birmingham. B45 8RS. Tel: 0121 457 6211. Email: membership@mail.nasuwt.org.uk

National Council for Mother Tongue Teaching (NCMTT), 5 Musgrave Crescent, London SW6 4PT.

National Foundation for Educational Research (NFER),The Mere, Upton Park, Slough, Berkshire SL1 2DQ. Tel: 01753 574123. Fax: 01753 691632. E-mail: enquiries@nfer.ac.uk

National Language Unit of Wales (NLUW) WJEC, 245 Western Avenue, Cardiff, South Glamorgan CF5 2YX. Tel: 01222 265007.

National Literacy Association (NLA), Office No 1, The Magistrates Court, Bargates, Christchurch, Dorset BH23 1PY. Tel: 01202 484 079. E-mail: nla@argonet.co.uk Website: http://www.nla.org.uk

Northern Ireland Council for the Curriculum, Examinations and Assessment (NICCEA), Beechill House, 42 Beechill Road, Belfast BT8 4RS. Tel: (028) 9033 5955. Fax: (028) 9032 6571. Email: NICILT@qub.ac.uk

OFSTED (Office for Standards in Education), Alexandra House, 29–33 Kingsway, London WC2B 6SE. Tel: 020 7421 6800 (download OFSTED reports on schools).

Panjabi Language Development Board (PLDB), Contact: S S Kalra, Hon. Secretary, 2 St Anne's Close, Handsworth Wood, Birmingham B20 1BS. Tel: 0121 551 5272. Fax: 0121 551 5272.

Professional Association of Teachers (PAT), 2 St James' Court, Friar Gate, Derby, DE1 1BT. Tel: 01332 372337 (PAT). Fax: 01332 290310/292431.

Qualifications and Curriculum Authority (QCA), 83 Piccadilly, London W1J 8QA Tel: 020 7509 5555. Fax: 020 7509 6666.

The Refugee Council. Website: http://www.refugeecouncil.org.uk

Resource Centre for Multicultural Education, Leicester, Forest Lodge Education Centre, Charnor Road, Leicester LE3 6LH. Tel: 0116 231 3399. Fax: 0116 231 1804. Jointly funded by Leicester City Council and Leicestershire County Council. Same address for Leicester MELAS (Minority Ethnic Language and Achievement Service).

Resource Unit for Supplementary and Mother-tongue Schools, Contact: Mohammed Abdelrazak, Director, 15 Great St Thomas Apostle, Mansion House, London EC4V 2BB. Tel: 020 7329 0815. Fax: 020 7329 0816. E-mail: resourceunit@netscapeonline.co.uk

Save the Children Centre for Young Children's Rights, Contact: Judy Gough, Information Worker, 356 Holloway Road, London N7 6PA. Tel: 020 7700 8127. Fax: 020 7697 0982. Email: cycr@scfuk.org.uk

Schofield and Sims Ltd, Dogley Mill, Fenay Bridge, Huddersfield HD8 0NQ. Tel: 01484 607 080. Fax: 01484 606 815. E-mail: sales@schofieldandsims.-co.uk Website: http://www.schofieldandsims.co.uk Welcome poster in over 20 languages and other materials.

The Schools' Arabic Project (SAP), Contact: Mr C J Gold, Dulwich College, Dulwich Common, London SE21 7LD. Tel: 020 8693 3601 (switchboard). Fax: 020 8693 6319. E-mail: goldcj@dulwich.org.uk

The Sikh Missionary Society, UK, 10 Featherstone Road, Southall, Middlesex, UB2 5AA. Tel: 020 8574 1902. Fax: 020 8574 1912.

The Stationery Office Ltd (previously HMSO), PO Box 276, London SW8 5DT.

Teacher Training Agency (TTA) Portland House, Stag Place, London SW1E 5TT. Tel: 020 7925 3700. E-mail: tta@gtnet.gov.uk

Universities Admissions Service (UCAS), Rosehill, New Barn Lane, Cheltenham, Gloucestershire, GL52 3LZ. Tel: 01242 222444. E-mail: enq@ucas.ac.uk

University of Cambridge Local Examinations Syndicate (UCLES). See OCR.

Universities Council for the Education of Teachers (UCET), 58 Gordon Square, London WC1H 0NT. E-mail: r.klassen@ioe.ac.uk

Welsh Joint Education Committee (WJEC), 245 Western Ave, Cardiff CF5 2YX. Tel: 0222 571101

Welsh Office Education Department, Crown Building, Cathays Park, Cardiff CF1 3NQ. Tel: 01222 825 111.

Scotland

The educational system in Scotland is different and separate from that in England and Wales.

The Dyslexia Institute (Scotland), Dyslexia Scotwest, 74 Victoria Crescent Road, Dowan Hill, Glasgow G12 9JN.

Scottish Consultative Council on the Curriculum (Scottish CCC), Gardyne Road, Dundee DD5 1NY. Tel: 01382 455053.

Scottish Council for Educational Technology (SCET), 74 Victoria Crescent Road, Glasgow G12 9JN. Tel: 0141 337 5000.

The Scottish Dyslexia Association, Unit 3, Stirling Business Centre, Wellgreen, Stirling FK8 2DZ.

The Scottish Dyslexia Trust, 16 Hope Street, Edinburgh EH2 4DD.

Scottish Executive Education Department (SEED), Education Department Secretariat, The Scottish Executive Area, 3-D Victoria Quay, Edinburgh EH6 6QQ Tel: 0131 244 1479. Fax: 0131 244 7122/23. E-mail: ceu@scotland.gov.uk

Scottish Qualifications Authority (SQA). Glasgow: Hanover House, 24 Douglas Street, Glasgow G2 7NQ, Scotland. Tel: 0141 248 7900. Fax: 0141 242 22440. **Dalkeith**: Ironmills Road, Dalkeith, Midlothian EH22 1LE, Scotland. Tel: 0131 663 6601. Fax: 0131 654 2664. For general enquiries contact helpdesk. Tel: 0141-242 2214. Email: helpdesk@sqa.org.uk

Eire

ADD/ADULT Family Support Group, 11 Summerfield Grn, Blanchardstown D15.

AHEAD (The Association for Higher Education Access and Disability), Newman House, 86 St. Stephen's Green, Dublin 2. Website: www.ahead.ie

Aontas (National Association of Adult Education), 22 Earlsfort Terrace, Dublin 2. Website: www.aontas.com

ASPIRE (The Asperger Syndrome Assocaiton of Ireland), 85 Woodley Park, Kilmacud, D 14.

Association for Children and Adults with Learning Disabilities, Anne Hughes, Suffolk Chambers, 1 Suffolk Street, Dublin 2

Authentik, 27 Westland Square, Dublin 2, Ireland.

Bord Iascaigh Mhara, POBox 12, Crofton Road, Dun Laoghaire, Co. Dublin. Website: www.bim.ie

Central Applications Office, Tower House, Eglinton Street, Galway. Website: www.cao.ie (Processes applications for entry to most undergraduate courses.)

Conference of Heads of Irish Universities, 10, Lower. Mount St., Dublin, 2 . Website: www.chiu.ie

Council of Directors – Institutes of Technology, 4 Lower Hatch St., Dublin 2. Web: www.councilofdirectors.ie

Department of Education & Science, Higher Education Section, Block 1, Floor 4, Irish Life Centre, Lower Abbey Street, Dublin 1.
Website: www.education.ie

Department of Education, Special Education Section, Principal Officer, Athlone, Co. Westmeath.

Dublin Institute for Advanced Studies, 10, Burlington Rd., Dublin, 4. Website: www.dias.ie

The Dyspraxia Association, 47 Mount Eagle Drive, Leopardstown Heights, Sandyford, D 18.

Expert Group on Future Skills Needs, Forfás, Wilton Park House, Wilton Place, Dublin 2. Website: www.skillsireland.ie

FÁS, The Training & Employment Authority, 27–33 Upper Baggot Street, Dublin 4. Website: www.fas.ie

Forbairt, Glasnevin, Dublin 9. (Promotion of indigenous industry/science and technology.)

Forfás, Wilton Park House, Wilton Place, Dublin, 2. Website: www.forfas.ie

Further Education and Training Awards Council, (FETAC), East Point Plaza, Dublin, 3. Website: www.fetac.ie

HEAnet, Brooklawn House, Crampton Ave., Shelbourne Rd., Dublin 4. Website: www.heanet.ie

HEDCO (Higher Education for Development Co-operation), IPC House, 35–39 Shelbourne Road, Ballsbridge, Dublin 4. Website: www.educationireland.ie

Higher Education Authority, 3rd Floor, Marine House, Clanwilliam Court, Dublin 2. Website: www.hea.ie

Higher Education and Training Awards Council, 26–27 Denzille Lane, Dublin 2. Website: www.hetac.ie

Hyperactive/Attention Deficit Disorder, 25 Lawnswood Park, Stillorgan, Co. Dublin.

ICOS (Irish Council for International Students), 541 Morehampton Road, Dublin 4. Website: www.icosirl.ie

IFUT (Irish Federation of University Teachers), 11 Merrion Square, Dublin 2. Website: www.ifut.ie

International Education Board of Ireland, IPC House, 35/39 Shelbourne Rd. Dublin 4. Website: www.educationireland.ie

Institiúid Teangeolaíochta Éireann, 31, Plás Mhic Liam, Baile Átha Cliath, 2. Website: www.ite.ie

Irish Association of Teachers in Special Education, The Teacher's Centre, Drumcondra, Dublin 9.

Irish Council for Science, Technology and Innovation, Wilton Park House, Wilton Place, Dublin, 2. Website: www.forfas.ie/icsti

Irish National Teachers Organisation, 35 Parnell Square, Dublin 1.

Irish Research Council for Science, Engineering and Technology, Brooklawn House, Crampton Ave., Shelbourne Rd., Dublin 4. Website: www.ircset.ie

The Irish Society of Autism, 16/17 Lr. O'Connell Street, Dublin 1.

The Minister of Education & Science, Marlboro Street, Dublin 1.

National Adult Literacy Agency, 76 Lower Gardiner Street, Dublin 1, Ireland. E-mail: nala@iol.ie

Special Education Section, Primary Branch, Department of Education, Athlone, Co. Westmeath.

The Netherlands

ACCESS (Administrative Committee to Coordinate English-Speaking Services), Plein 24, NL-2511 CS, The Hague.

Parents United for children who learn differently, American School of The Hague, Rijksstraatweg 200, NL-2242 BX Wassenaar.

Stichting C.S.N. (Children with Special Needs), Jim Taylor, Dr. Schaepmanlaan 4, NL-2251 AV Noordwijkerhout.

USA

Barton Reading & Spelling System, 2059 Camden Avenue, Suite 186, San Jose, CA 95124.

Children and Adults with Attention Deficit Disorders (CH.A.D.D.), 499

Northwest 70th Avenue, Suite 308, Plantation, Florida 33317. Website: http://oneaddplace.com

The Council for Exceptional Children, 1920 Association Drive, Reston, VA 20191-1589.

The International Dyslexia Association, 8600 LaSalle Road, Chester Building, Suite #382 Baltimore, Maryland 21286-2044.

Learning Disabilities Association of America, 4156 Library Road, Pittsburgh, PA 15234. Website: http://ldanal.org/

National Association for Bilingual Education, USA (NABE). Website: http://www.nabe.org

National Center for Learning Disabilities, 99 Park Avenue New York, NY 10016. Website: http://www.ncld.org/

National Information Center for Children and Youth with Disabilities, POBox 1492, Washington, DC 20013-1492. Email: nichcy@aed.org

National Institute on Deafness and Other Communication Disorders, National Institutes of Health, 31 Center Drive, MSC 2320, Bethesda, MD USA 20892-2320.

Office of Special Education, US Department of Education, Switzer Building, 330 C Street, SW, Room 3132, Washington, DC 20202-2524. Website: http://www.ed.gov/

Dyslexia, dyspraxia and special needs organisations

Adult Dyslexia Organization, 336 Brixton Road, London, SW9 7AA. E-mail: dyslexia.hq@dial.pipex.com

The British Dyslexia Association, 98 London Road, Reading RG1 5AU. E-mail: (helpline): info@dyslexiahelp-bda.demon.co.uk E-mail (admin): admin@b-da-dyslexia.demon.co.uk This association represents over two million dyslexic children and adults. They have a list of support groups and contacts world-wide and offer books and pamphlets like, *A Survival Kit: Preventing Parental Burn-Out, A Young Person's Guide to Dyslexia*, and *Handwriting Helpline*. There is a special selection for teachers at all levels.

Children with Special Needs, American Women of Berkshire & Surrey, c/o Fred Evans, Pineacre Cottage, Sunning Avenue, Sunningdale, Berkshire SL5 9QE

Dyslexia Computer Resource Centre, Department of Psychology, University of Hull, Hull HU6 7RX. E-mail: dyslexia@hull.ac.uk

The Dyslexia Institute, 133 Gresham Road, Staines, Middlesex TW18 2AJ.

Dyspraxia Foundation, West Alley, Hitchin, Herts SG5 1EG.

Learning Assessment Centre, 44 Springfield Road, Horsham, West Sussex RH 12 2PD. Specialises in assessment and treatment of attention deficit/hyperactivity disorders.

Index

A levels, 16
accelerated learning, 20
activities, 23, 44, 45
administration, 70
aims of the department, 4
alkali metals, 62, 63
AppleMac computers, 73
Applied Science, 15
assessment, 16, 57, 58, 67
astronomy, 16
attainment levels, 12, 13

BBC Bitesize revision, 64
biology, 17
bodily-kinaesthetic learners, 30
book boxes, 52, 56

career entry profile, 65
CASE, 13
chemistry, 17
classroom discipline plan, 32, 37
combined science, 3
commendation, 34
computers in science, 73
consistency, 35, 39
Co-ordinated Science, 14
curriculum, 2

datalogging, 74
detention, 35, 37, 38
demonstration, 60, 61
development plan, 5
diary, 52, 55
digital brain, 76
differentiation, 23
discipline, 32, 45
Double Award, 14

electronics, 16
emotional intelligence, 16
expectations, 9, 22, 32, 39

feedback, 21
fieldwork, 9
filing, 52, 54, 56

GCSE, 3
geology, 16
gifted and talented, 28
GNVQ, 18
graph package, 75

health and safety, 9, 45, 47, 61, 63
hierarchy, 1
homework, 35
house points, 34

ICT, 10, 65, 73
induction tutor, 66
induction year, 65, 66
initial teacher training, 65
interpersonal intelligence, 30
intrapersonal intelligence, 30
Internet, 74
interviews, 71
IQ, 28

key skills, 10
Key Stage 3, 2, 8, 12, 28, 69, 74
  strategy, 9
Key Stage 4, 2, 14, 69

laboratory rules, 33
learning, 26, 27
lesson objectives, 41

lesson plan, 23, 48, 50
life processes and living things, 12
linguistic intelligence, 29
literacy, 9, 10, 28
Local Education Authority, 63, 67
logical/mathematical intelligence, 29

mark book, 52, 53, 54
marking, 57
materials and their properties, 12
meetings, 68
mixed ability, 2
moderation, 14
Modular Science, 14
monitoring, 68
multiple intelligences, 29
musical intelligence, 30

National Curriculum, 2, 8, 13
naturalistic intelligence, 30
numeracy, 10, 28

objectives (lesson), 41, 42, 43
observation, 67

PANDA, 13
parents' evenings, 72
pending file, 52, 55
performance management, 68
physical processes, 12
physics, 18
planner, 52, 53, 54
plenary, 46
policies, 4, 6
post, 51
Powerpoint, 76
praise, 34, 39
preparation, 58
prior learning, 9
professional development, 67, 68
programmes of study, 8, 12
promotion, 2

QCA scheme of work, 6, 12, 19
questioning, 23, 24, 44

rationale, 4
referral, 38, 71
relaxation, 21
reports, 71
resources, 9, 41
revision, 74
rewards, 33, 35

sanctions, 35, 39
SATs, 13
scheme of work, 6, 12, 19, 52, 55
scientific enquiry, 12
sensors, 75
setting, 3
simulations, 74
Single Award, 15
sixth form, 16
spatial intelligence, 30
spreadsheets, 75
Standard Attainment Tasks, 13
starters, 41, 43
streaming, 3
syllabus, 26

target setting, 10
teacher training, 65
team building, 21
technicians, 1, 41
testing, 59
thinking skills, 10
three-part lesson, 41, 62
threshold, 69
time management, 57
timetables, 5
to-do list, 52, 55
Triple Award, 15
tutor group, 70, 71

units of work, 8, 9